WILD STORIES *from the* IRISH UPLANDS

# WILD STORIES

### *from the*

# IRISH UPLANDS

## John G. O'Dwyer

CURRACH
BOOKS

First published in 2019 by

 **CURRACH**BOOKS

23 Merrion Square
Dublin 2, Ireland
www.currachbooks.com

ISBN: 9781782189121

Set in Freight Text Pro 10.5/14
Cover illustration and book design by Alba Esteban | Currach Books
Printed by ScandBook. Falun

*To Carmel, Aoife and Caoimhe*

# Contents

# Reference Map

# Introduction

A n old farmer once told me that mountains are just land that's a bit up in the air. In Ireland, we certainly have a considerable amount of terrain that is "a bit up in the air" but not really that far up. You see, it is possible in favourable weather for those of us who are moderately fit to reach any Irish mountaintop in a day's hike. All we have to do is select the least challenging route and then do nothing more technical than putting one foot in front of the other. In truth, there is something about unchallenging uplands that draws us to them and makes us want to reach the highest point. I remember feeling this urge in spades when I first gazed upon the mistily seductive slopes of the Galtee Mountains from my home in Co. Tipperary. No doubt this most human of desires has been common to up-gazing people throughout history.

We can safely assume, therefore, that the Irish uplands have been accessed since the dawn of human history and, it is small wonder then, that these highlands did not become distant objects of reverence and fear. This was the case with the forbidding tops of some of the world's great mountains, such as the Matterhorn, K2 and Everest. Unknown and untrodden, these peaks were feared by the surrounding communities as the abode of monsters and evil deities. In contrast, the vertically unassuming Irish mountains were known and oft-visited, and so they became a reassuring and accessible aspect of the landscape. Soon they were being purposefully woven into legend, for a salient peak above us is a universal presence that all of us relate to. Its constant, comforting reality builds local identity and nurtures the enabling mythologies that are necessary for us to create strong bonds within our communities.

People have mostly had recourse to the uplands in times of change, challenge or combat. Ireland's turbulent history has ensured that almost all the defining eras of Ireland's past have been represented by events in the high country. The world-famous Burren of County Clare comes replete with the fascinating stone forts built in high places for the protection of their families and livestock by early farmers. Ulster held out longest as the last bastion of Gaelic Ireland because it was defended by a necklace of mountains and bogs to the south of the province. After the failure of the 1798 Rising, it was in the Wicklow Mountains that the most defiant rebels found sanctuary. The challenge of a rapidly growing population in pre-Famine Ireland forced many families into the uplands to seek additional land on which to eke out a precarious existence. The remains of the lazy beds in which they grew potatoes are to this day a common sight in the Irish hill country.

It was in mountainous areas of counties Tipperary and Cork that opposition to British rule in Ireland was most veracious during the War of Independence, while at the end of the Irish Civil War the final redoubts of Republicanism were to be found within upland communities from Sligo to Waterford and Kerry to Armagh. So, let us now set out together on a journey that follows the ebb and flow of times gone by as enacted in the high country.

We will find it was the land clearing efforts of Stone Age farmers that were partially responsible for creating the Burren. Early writers wishing to build the mythology of St Patrick were, we will discover, careful to continually link Ireland's national apostle to the spiritual dominance of lofty places. One result was an early Christian pilgrimage to Croagh Patrick's summit that flourishes to this day. In West Kerry, the highest mountain on the Dingle Peninsula was, after his death, dedicated by mythology to Saint Brendan. When a couple of Ulster princes escaped from Dublin Castle, they didn't make a bee-line northeast across the flat, but exposed, Central Plain of Ireland towards home. Instead, they headed south to the relative security of the Wicklow Mountains. This was the nearest place to Dublin where the English writ did not run, for it was a general rule of the time that Queen Elizabeth experienced the most profound difficulties when trying to impose her will on Ireland's upland areas.

Outlaws and rapparees in the 18th Century used an intimate knowledge of these same uplands to stay a step ahead of the English rulers and thereby built a cache of support among ordinary people. Young Irelander and Fenian revolutionaries employed the great symbolism of mountaintop mass meetings to mobilise the populace against perceived oppression, while Cistercian monks sought the opposite: a return to contemplative solitude on the silent slopes of the Knockmealdown Mountains.

After the Soloheadbeg Ambush of 1919 resulted in the death of two police constables, the initial impulse of volunteers Séamus Robinson, Seán Treacy and Dan Breen was to seek sanctuary among the snow-laden slopes of the Galtee Mountains. Later, Breen found refuge in a small cave in the same mountains. Similarly, it was to the embrace of upland communities that rebel fighters Tom Barry and Liam Lynch retreated when the lowlands became untenable for their cause.

Things are, of course, never just normal in Ireland, it's not the way we do things: instead, our nation is invariably either in the grip of a boom or a bust. Whatever the economic conditions however, the number of hillwalkers continued to grow rapidly as Ireland urban-ized and industrialized in the second half of the 20th Century. The reason for the uninterrupted growth may be that in a recession there is more time available to enjoy the outdoors and also more need for escape, while in good times additional people can afford the cost of trips away to the hills.

It was certainly true that by the time I tiptoed into hillwalking in the late 20th Century, the Irish hill country had morphed from a place of refuge and conflict to a playground for ramblers and climbers. Pilgrims were also taking again to the ancient pilgrim paths as part of both an outer and inner journey while rock-climbers were discovering new features and routes that were previously unknown. Later, we all marvelled at a Californian wonder boy of Irish ancestry. On his frequent Irish visits, he defied death on a daily basis while stylishly pushing back the frontiers of the possible as he scaled Ireland's most vertical mountain and coastal crags.

All this meant that safety in the uplands became a new concern for the hordes of Irish people and overseas visitors participating in outdoor recreation. Descending from the summit of Carrauntoohil almost 25 years ago, I had my first encounter with a mountain accident. From the unforgiving heights of Primroses Ridge came the successive 3 blasts of a whistle that indicated someone was in trouble. We made our way up beneath the ridge and there shouted to one of two climbers who had been hit by a rockfall; the other climber was unconscious.

This was clearly a job for a rescue team and, surprisingly for those times, a couple of our party possessed mobile phones that actually worked. Within an hour Kerry Mountain Rescue Team were on the scene and soon after, two of their members had calmly ascended to a point just beneath the climbers. From here, they guided in a helicopter that winched the climbers to safety and a full recovery in hospital. This constituted the first ever successful airlift from the Northeast face of Carrrauntoohil.

It left me with a lasting admiration for a team of volunteers that, from humble beginnings based upon tragedies in the 1960s, became a sophisticated and highly trained search and rescue organization. Over the years members of Kerry Mountain Rescue Team have dedicated themselves to ensuring that the timeless tradition of accessing the magnificent Southwest uplands continues in the safest possible manner. As this area became a Mecca for outdoor pursuits, the sometimes-epic efforts of these volunteers to save lives among the country's highest peaks makes for yet another fascinating saga.

It shouldn't, therefore, come as a surprise that each era from Ireland's story has been reflected by happenings in the hill country. Over 30 years of walking through the uplands I have heard many first-hand accounts of these events from local people and on occasion been regaled with the poignant songs of loss and emigration that come down to us from the hill country. The universal truism I have gleaned from these accounts is that upland people form a particularly strong attachment to their own place – they may leave it but it rarely leaves them.

The other truism is that those holding the high ground invariably possess a valuable psychological advantage. Throughout history, successive generations have striven to control the highest places, for they were well aware that with elevation came power and control. It is truly inescapable. No matter where we wander among the highlands of Ireland, we find history has loaded our most elevated places with unforgettable stories and captivating legends. It has also lauded them in song and story, for through the ages the uplands have been inextricably intertwined with the ebb and flow of Irish history.

# CHAPTER 1

# In the Footsteps of a Saint

Nobody else has influenced Irish lives so profoundly. Celebrated in more countries than any other, his feast day has morphed into an international event that involves the greening of hundreds of the world's most iconic locations. Andrew, George and David, the saintly men of Ireland's nearest neighbours, hardly get a look in by comparison, while this country's national apostle has gone mega, becoming the world's most commercially exploited saint.

St Patrick's Day has morphed into a global behemoth, an international goodwill fest for Ireland, of almost inestimable PR value. It is at this time our diaspora extravagantly strut their stuff, reminding others not fortunate enough to have ancestors from the Emerald Isle of their own luck at being Irish. Yet, we understand little about the individual behind the extravaganza as the cult of sainthood has, as is often the case, hugely obscured the person.

From his own words written in Latin, we know Patrick was the son of a wealthy Christian living in Britain. Aged 16, he was captured by Irish raiders as the terminally weakened Roman Empire was no longer able to defend its borders. If his personal account is true - there is no collaborating evidence - he was then sold to slavery in Ireland. During this period, he became increasingly religious and turned to long periods of prayer. After six years, he experienced a religious epiphany while tending flocks and believed God was calling him home. Motivated to escape he fled for 200 miles, which in pre-historic Ireland would have been, for a penniless, escaping slave, a considerable accomplishment in itself, that would probably require some divine intervention. He then found a ship that conveyed him away from Ireland. After many difficulties, including becoming lost in a wilderness, he eventually returned to his family. Later, he studied Christianity and following an apparition, which suggested the Irish people were calling him back, he returned to Ireland as a bishop and was instrumental in converting the island to the new faith.

It is, of course, almost inconceivable that Patrick came to an island that had not previously been exposed to the Christian faith. The Roman Empire had, after all, been Christianised by the Emperor Constantine more than a century before his arrival and Ireland had particularly strong trade links with Britain. Simple narratives are, of course, the most powerful, so the early Irish Church cannily promoted the first bishop of the dominant See of Armagh in a series of hagiologies. St Patrick, who has never been formally canonised as a saint, was entirely credited with converting the people of Ireland to Christianity. This served the purpose of making Armagh the most important Irish bishopric, while other contemporary saints and important Christian missionaries such as Declan and Ailbe were condemned to relative obscurity.

Outside of these predisposed writings, facts are scant about this British born saint who has come to be regarded as quintessentially Irish. Mythology compensates, however, with a wonderfully colourful Patrician narrative. Often depicted as carrying a cross in one hand and a shamrock in the other, Patrick came to Ireland at a time when the Irish language did not possess a written alphabet and so an expansive oral mythology evolved around Ireland's national apostle. This was initially passed on in the spoken word from generation to generation as a series of richly embroidered stories. It is sometimes said these myths from the past are always true, for they accurately reflect human aspiration at a particular point in history. So, let us now set out on our magical and mythical journey in the highly mythologised footsteps of Ireland's patron saint. It will take us on a mostly upland adventure through the north, midlands and west before concluding at his reputed resting place in Downpatrick.

Inevitably, we begin with the hill that is forever associated with Patrick. Lying about 35 miles north of Belfast, this scene-stealing summit of Slemish is the focal point of a pilgrimage on March 17. According to tradition, Patrick was enslaved to Milchu and worked as a herdsman on the slopes of Slemish, Co. Antrim. Perhaps it was here he came to understand the powerful symbolism of high places, for the Irish uplands would become a lifelong obsession. Certainly, it is a great place to start our pilgrim journey.

The short but enthralling 30-minute climb allows dreamy views over the mythical north-east. It is quite steep, however, and careful scrambling is required to overcome some of the obstacles. Once there you will doubtless be surprised to find the summit remains as bare as it was in the time of Patrick. It is certain that if this iconic hill were located in the south of Ireland and not at the heart of non-conformist Ulster, there would be at least a Holy Year cross and, perhaps, a magisterial statue of Patrick crowning the top.

Now, we head south through the red brick sprawl of Belfast city, a place where, we might reflect, the religion introduced by Patrick to Ireland has had much to answer for, with the Christianisation of Ireland seeming hereabouts something of an unfinished business. Then, it is onward through the Drumlin rich County Down countryside to Saul. Legend holds that strong winds swept Patrick's boat into Strangford Lough, as he returned on his Irish mission in the year 432. Landing at Saul, on what by any standards was a dangerous mission aimed at subverting Irish paganism, he cannily got the local chief Dichu onside by immediately converting him. His hard-won competence in the Irish language was, you will probably agree, an essential selling point here. He was also granted a barn by the newly Christianised Dichu, which then became Ireland's first church. After visiting the 20th Century Celtic revival chapel and round tower, we will follow the Stations of the Cross on a 20-minute hike to the crest of Patrick's Hill. Here, we gaze upon the world's tallest statue of the apostle, which was carved from the local Mourne granite. But even without this novel inducement, the climb is worthwhile. On a clear day, we will enjoy the added bonus of magnificent views over Strangford Lough and the Mourne Mountains.

Next, we follow in Patrick's footsteps as he crosses a pass between the Cooley Mountains and the famous Ring Dyke of Slieve Gullion. Ulster is protected to the south by a ring of mountains and moorlands, but there is a chink in these defences. It's known as the Gap of the North and this defile has been the main conduit for warring armies entering and leaving Ulster since the time of the fabled warrior Cuchulainn. In Patrick's time, it was situated on the royal road leading south from the seat of the kings of Ulster at Emain Macha.

Beyond the Gap, Patrick entered the rich, well-watered lands of what is now Co. Meath, where he faced his first big test. It was essential that the Irish High King, who reigned on the Hill of Tara, should come on board with the Christian faith and so this is the place where we interrogate one of the best-known Patrician mythologies.

With heroic – or as most of us would think – foolhardy indifference to the protocols of royalty, Patrick went about the process of ingratiating himself in a most unusual way by immediately defying the King. Ascending the nearby Hill of Slane, he broke all custom and precedent by lighting a pascal flame in advance of King Laoghaire's fire at Tara celebrating the Bealtaine Festival. At this point, we will likely agree that if either of us did this, our heads would not remain long in contact with our bodies. Be reassured, however; Patrician mythology comes without such myth-busting consequences. Apparently, the reckless act – which should have peremptorily ended Patrick's mission – in its audacity made an unexpectedly favourable impression on the King.

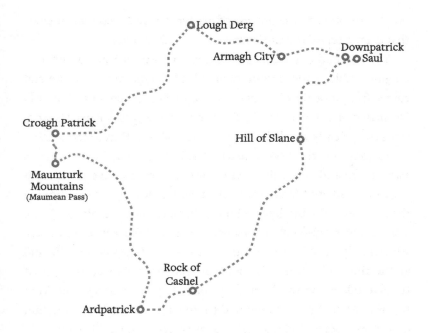

According to tradition, Laoghaire's soldiers were unable to extinguish Patrick's fire. Recognising the great power of the Saint, the King allowed his subjects convert to Christianity but did not do so himself. St Erc, who was first at Tara to pay homage to Patrick, then founded a monastery on the Hill of Slane. The symbolism was clear: Patrick had triumphed over paganism and soon a tsunami of piety extinguished Druidic beliefs forever from Ireland as monotheism arrived to stay.

The saint's message was, nevertheless, a subversive one. In a time when, according to societal ideals, the most revered heroes should display superhuman levels of strength and fearlessness, Patrick was a social disrupter who preached instead humility and meekness and that all are equal before one God. This message was always likely to ruffle some feathers and, according to the Saint's own account, there were a few scrapes with authority along the way. Overall, however, the evangelisation of Ireland was accomplished with relative ease and without notable recourse to the process of martyrdom and sectarian violence that characterised the Christianisation of other lands.

You will find our ascent to the upland north of Slane an unchallenging amble. A ten-minute ramble leads to the monastic site and ruined friary atop the hill, while to the west, are the remains of an early Norman motte. Here you will discover that one part of Patrick's story rings true; clearly visible is the Hill of Tara about 16km to the south.

It may surprise you to learn at this stage that in the time of Patrick, Ireland was well provided for with roads. Five great royal highways radiated from Tara with a series of lesser roads linking these. This undoubtedly facilitated Patrick's mission, although the saint is never depicted on horseback in his spiritual representations, which really would have been the sensible way to get around Ireland at the time. Whatever his mode of transport, Patrick is reputed to have taken the south-easterly road (Slige Cualann) from Tara towards what is now Dublin and there baptised the local chieftain on the spot where today stands the great cathedral in his name.

Somewhere on his evangelical journey through the Dublin area, he is believed to have encountered legendary Irish warrior Oisín who had just returned to Ireland having spent 300 years in the land of eternal youth with Niamh of the Golden Hair. Whether Patrick questioned the wisdom of abandoning such a legendary beauty as Niamh for a return to Ireland we are not told, but Oisín was not one of Patrick's success stories - he refused to accept the new religion and died while still a pagan.

Mythology also speaks of Patrick explaining the mystery of three persons in one God to an unbeliever by showing him that the three-leaved shamrock has just one stalk. This was a less than perfect explanation of the Holy Trinity, but then Patrick never claimed to be faultless or all-knowing, stating in his own humble words "My name is Patrick. I am a sinner, a simple country person, and the least of all believers."

After Dublin, the Saint is likely to have followed the most southerly of the royal roads (Slige Dála) as he made his way to Munster. It would first have led him to where the town of Naas is now situated, before swinging sharply southwest for Cashel of the Kings. On our 21st Century journey, we will eschew the mayhem of Dublin by heading directly into the south midlands and uphill again, this time to the high point of a limestone escarpment, where resided Aenghus, King of Munster.

Throughout his Irish mission Patrick demonstrated a useful knack for immediately getting the local leadership on his side and it was at the Rock of Cashel that he brought off his greatest coup. The saint baptised Aenghus while carelessly impaling the royal foot with the point of his crozier during the ceremony. Again, this might have got you or me into any amount of hot water, but not Patrick. Thinking it was all part of the ceremony, Aenghus didn't complain and instead became Ireland's first Christian king.

We will have a great time pottering around the truly awe-inspiring buildings on the Rock of Cashel including the 13th Century St Patrick's Cathedral and Cormac's Chapel, which is the outstanding jewel in the crown of Hiberno-Romanesque architecture that has recently been restored. None of the buildings date from Patrician times, but the highly professional guided tour will give a great insight into the later history of the Rock. You will learn that the place became an important ecclesiastical centre in the 12th Century, when the site was donated to the Church by the King of Munster, and it continued thus until 1749 when the cold, drafty buildings on the exposed summit were abandoned. Arthur Price, the Anglican Archbishop of Cashel had, during this period, begun building a new cathedral and a more comfortable residence in the town that at the time of writing was being developed as a luxury hotel. Almost forgotten for a couple of centuries, the abandoned buildings on the Rock eventually morphed into one of Ireland's best-known and most popular visitor attractions.

The highlight of the tour comes, however, in the unlikely form of one Archbishop Miler Magrath – a character who today would be a tabloid editor's dream. A long-lived Franciscan monk of the 16th and 17th centuries, he soon eschewed the troublesome encumbrance of his chastity and poverty vows by marrying and then managing for nine years to successfully ride two episcopal horses. Destined to be a headline-grabber if alive today, he was dogged throughout his life by stories that would now make excellent tabloid fodder: rumours abounded of extramarital sex, ill-gotten gains and religious hypocrisy. Certainly, he was a pluralist, becoming archbishop to the Protestant diocese of Cashel, while simultaneously managing to remain Catholic bishop of the Ulster Down and Connor diocese for a period of nine years. A favourite of Queen Elizabeth I, if not of Pope Gregory XIII, he was ultimately excommunicated from the Catholic Church and thus deprived of the income stream from Down and Connor. Unabashed, the politically astute Miler compensated by adding the Anglican diocese of Waterford and Lismore, and later Killala and Achonry to his considerable income stream from Church endowments.

Probably not that excessive by the duplicitous standards of his day, Miler managed, somewhere along the way, to earn the tabloid-style sobriquet "Scoundrel of Cashel", which sealed his faith. As the convenient local fall guy, he proves an invaluable "pantomime villain" on most guided tours of the Rock. Standing beside his tomb in the great roofless cathedral of St Patrick before an expectant mass of visitors, it is understandably difficult for the guides to resist dipping into the lurid but highly embellished tales of his unconventional lifestyle.

In contrast to the supposedly unblemished life of Patrick, accounts of Milers legendary fecundity - featuring several concubines and a host of illegitimate offspring - are almost guaranteed to raise a wry laugh. This is especially true if the troublesome fact that such excesses were commonplace in the Tudor period is conveniently glossed over. One thing is certain, however, Miler was one of the most accomplished and long-lived survivors in Irish history, seeing off four English monarchs during his lifetime, including the long reigning Elizabeth. His extended and lavishly unconventional bishopric at Cashel certainly does much to upstage the more sedate story of Patrick's earlier visit to the Rock. Don't be surprised, therefore, if your guided tour pays close attention to Miler and his misdeeds while generally being more parsimonious on details about the national apostle.

Now things get a bit political as they are wont to do in Ireland. In the Deise of Co. Waterford, St Declan already held powerful sway. Consecrated a bishop in Rome, he had returned and preached the gospel in his native Waterford at a time that, many historians believe, was prior to Patrick's arrival in 432AD. It was imperative that noses remained in joint, so Patrick emphasised his own dominance by confirming Declan as Bishop of the Deise, after the Ardmore saint had journeyed by chariot to Cashel. Wisely, however, Patrick refrained from actually crossing the mountain passes into the Deise. This allowed Declan remain supreme in his south Munster heartland, which he continues to do to this day as the dominant and much venerated saint of Co. Waterford. The importance of this meeting at Cashel between two of Ireland's great apostles was recognised in 2019 with the waymarking and reopening of the route taken by the Waterford saint on his journey to meet Patrick. Known as St Declan's Way, it links the ancient royal seat of Munster with ecclesiastic Ardmore and is now one of Ireland's foremost pilgrim paths.

We don't follow this trail, however, but head west instead, to what is now Ardpatrick, Co. Limerick where our national apostle, true to previous form, ascended to the local highpoint. While he generally delegated the monastery building to those coming after him, Patrick rolled up his sleeves here. Legend proclaims he constructed his first monastic settlement atop this green and fertile hill, which thrived for many centuries afterward. Following the short but steep track to the monastic site that leads up from the eponymous village, you will undoubtedly marvel at the great panorama over the emerald patchwork of the Golden Vale misting away to the horizon. This is set against the stark backdrop of the Ballyhoura Mountains to the east and south. I think you will agree, there is a powerfully evocative sense of history here and with a little imagination you may fancy Pre-Christian farmers are still working in the fertile plains of the Golden Vale below. Small wonder, perhaps, that Patrick tarried a while here.

West of the Shannon now, which Patrick would have been obliged to cross by boat since bridge building in Ireland was still a long way behind the engineering standard of the Roman Empire. Then it is on to the Maumturk Mountains of Connemara. It is a long journey and you may wonder on the way at the phenomenal success that Patrick enjoyed with converting the Irish people. To shorten the road let me, therefore, expound upon my pet theory for this occurrence, which goes beyond the saint's facility with the Irish language. In essence, the pagan message stated that if you appeased the gods, they would help you in this life, otherwise they would destroy you. Christianity, by contrast, offered a unique and altogether more sophisticated selling point: a much better world to come where those who lived virtuous lives would be united with loved ones in heaven. It is a compelling and captivating vision mining into the deepest human desires, which the existing religions could not match. In modern marketing parlance paganism would be termed an inferior product – a Lada competing with a Rolls Royce.

You can now while away the time by thinking out your own theory for the success of the Christian mission to Ireland as we climb to the head of the Maumean Pass in the footsteps of our national apostle. Here, you will doubtless be intrigued to discover that a Pattern (pilgrimage to a site regarded as sacred) has taken place here since early Christian times.

Tradition holds that on reaching this high point, Patrick, observing the watery, boggy expanse of South Connemara did what I guess most of us would have done, he declined to go further. He did, however, Christianise the site when he blessed Connemara from the pass while conveniently keeping his feet dry. The Pattern later became extremely popular during penal times when there was no formal Catholic Church in Ireland and the practice of religion became highly informalised. As the Church struggled to become more formal in the 19th Century, efforts were made to suppress these practices and the Pattern at Maumean, like many others, was discontinued. It was, however, revived again in the 1980s and has continued ever since.

Maumean will prove an enjoyable day: a pleasant walk bearing many resonances from Ireland's Christian past. There are all the usual signatures of pilgrimage: an oratory, an outdoor altar, a rocky cleft where St Patrick reputedly slept (uncomfortably, it would appear) and a favours adorned holy well. Likely you will agree, however, that the main reward for this 1.5-hour upland ascent is the sublime vista east and west.

The idea of self-sacrifice is central to pilgrimage and we now move back to a time before the necessity of a walking journey was engineered out of our lives. We must lace up the hiking boots securely for things are about to get tougher on Ireland's holiest mountain. Bearing many resonances from its origins as a place of pagan worship, Croagh Patrick is a mountain that must surely have been surprised by its own extraordinary popularity. It is climbed about one hundred thousand times annually for it is reputedly the mountaintop on which St Patrick fasted for 40 days. Despite this hardship, he apparently remained in a mood to be helpful towards the people of Ireland for he took the time out from prayer and privation to banish all species of snake from the island. These days this might be considered a sinister assault on biodiversity and Patrick would probably have found himself extensively trolled on social media. But these were different times, it was the snakes that were considered sinister and Patrick's popularity rose steeply.

On the uncooperatively steep ascent you will probably conclude Patrick was indeed a tough cookie, with all the credentials to qualify him as Ireland's first mountain climber. The path is undoubtedly demanding, and will probably seem relentless as you plough upwards through rivers of scree. About half way up, the slope eases for a while at a point where it intersects with the Tochar Phádraig: the 35km pilgrim path from Ballintubber Abbey which is described in Chapter 10.

The toughest bit has still to come and as we tackle it, I am going to take your mind off the ascent by setting you a little challenge. Walking the pilgrim paths of Ireland while writing my previous book, a question occurred to me about what motivates people to go on pilgrimage. I mulled over this through many a long walk and finally the word "DARE" came into my head as an acronym for pilgrim motivation. Is it all about *discovery*, mainly personal self-discovery; *appreciation*, for a favour bestowed; *remembering*, a special person; or finally *escape*, when the pressures of life seem overwhelming? If you think the answer to this question is yes, you can now contemplate which of the above motivates you. If you think the answer is no, you can shorten the ascent by trying to figure out your own more accurate acronym.

After some huffing and puffing, the seemingly interminable upwards path will eventually meander to a conclusion. Immediately obvious on reaching the summit is the relatively modern and not noticeably attractive 20th Century chapel that is rather incongruously set on its rocky throne. Fear not, however, your efforts have not been wasted for the charm of this mountain lies not in the immediate but in the distant. On a clear day, we will view a landscape little altered since St Patrick reputedly trod these self-same stones. Majestic vistas open from the great sweep of multi-islanded Clew Bay to the pristine wildness of the Mayo Mountains and moorlands beyond.

Obviously, Patrick isn't feeling the best after his fast, so you will probably not be surprised that he refrains from climbing on his next visit, which is to Lough Derg, Co. Donegal. That doesn't mean he takes it easy however, for a fearsome serpent resides in the lake and must be slain. Serpent extermination is no problem to a saint, of course, but its blood stained the water, thus creating the appellation Lough Derg (the red lake). Patrick then visits Station Island where, in a cave, he is shown a vision of purgatory and is promised that those spending a day and a night here would be entirely purged of their sins. By the 12th Century, the cave, now known as St Patrick's Purgatory, had become a renowned place of pilgrimage for absolution seekers. It was one of the very few Irish locations denoted on medieval European maps with pilgrims coming from all over Western Europe and even from as far away as Hungary.

Our easy 12km pilgrimage follows in the footsteps of medieval penitents - not to Station Island, where pilgrims go today - but Saints Island, where existed a medieval monastery. Far removed from roads and modernity, you will enjoy this stroll for the many resonances from the area's pilgrim past. There is also the option of going for broke and returning to complete the immensely tough three-day Lough Derg Pilgrimage. Exactly as penitents from past generations have done, you would, with barefoot prayer, fasting and sleep deprivation, 'renounce the world, the flesh and the Devil'. It is a hard three days, but completing the toughest pilgrimage in Christendom, which takes place between June and August, should guarantee you a later meeting with St Patrick in paradise.

Apparently re-energised, Patrick next made his way to what is now Armagh City and, of course, laid claim to the highest point. With thoughts, perhaps, of finally hanging up his walking sandals, it was here he built a stone church in the place where the Protestant Cathedral now stands. According to tradition, he then proclaimed Armagh Ireland's holiest place and thus founded the See of Armagh and became its first bishop. To this day, the leading status of both the Protestant and Catholic Archbishops of Armagh is based on the belief that their episcopal See can be traced directly back to Patrick, making Armagh the ecclesiastical capital of Ireland. Certainly, it has long been in Armagh's interests to promote their first bishop above other claimants as the primary evangeliser of the Irish people.

You will discover that Armagh, the last resting place of renowned Irish High King Brian Ború, is one of Ireland's hidden gems. Visiting both the Catholic and Church of Ireland cathedrals, you will most certainly be captivated by the breath-taking views of the city.

The Irish Annals relate that, when close to death, Patrick was told by an angel to return to his original landing place at Saul. Having come full circle, he died here on March 17th, 461. The angel then returned and decreed Patrick's body be placed on an ox cart and buried where the oxen stopped. This was in Downpatrick, at a location which is now beside the magnificent Down Cathedral. No better place to end our journey than at nearby St Patrick's Centre. This multi-media presentation accurately charts the life of Patrick, drawing heavily on his own words to bring together the full Patrician story.

From his own writings, Patrick emerges as a man with all the doubts and perceived failings that afflict other mortals, particularly those who have been through a traumatic experience in early life. But, of course, we take from history what we want and Patrick has been transformed over the centuries into a wise and avuncular figure - the very personification of Irishness. The enduring popularity of Patrick through the centuries, when other saints have come and gone from fashion must surely arise from the fact that he is a rare unifying figure. For a grievously divided nation, he is a person to whom all beliefs and none can give full and unconditional allegiance. In that sense he has achieved what no other Irish leader has since managed to bring about.

# CHAPTER 2

# First Voyage to the New World?

A s he was about to begin, he realised he had forgotten something important. An unfortunate occurrence this, since he was standing on the summit of one of Ireland's highest mountains. Now, if this were to happen to you or me, there would be no help for it but a long and forlorn trudge to the mountain foot, but true saints are not afflicted by such trivial inconveniences. Gazing at the long line of pilgrims ascending the mountain in his wake, he turned to the nearest and said, "Get the missal". The pilgrim understood what was required and in a series of Chinese whispers, the message was relayed down the mountain. The prayer book was retrieved by the last person who, as luck would have it, was just setting out. Then, it was passed up to the summit of Mount Brandon so that St Brendan could begin celebrating mass in his oratory. Fact or myth, the retelling of this story appears to have a clear objective; its aim is surely to emphasise the importance of Brendan in the early Irish Christian Church and his huge popularity among the people of the Dingle Peninsula. Even in the avowedly secular world of today, this popularity remains undiminished.

Brendan, the patron saint of County Kerry, was born in Annagh, near present-day Fenit, Co. Kerry in the 5th Century. From his birthplace he could gaze out across the mysterious ocean, with the Dingle Peninsula pointing tantalisingly, like a great index finger, to the west. This fact is today commemorated by a very impressive hilltop statue at Fenit Harbour which shows the saint pointing resolutely west and past Mount Brandon to the New World. What you might at first find surprising about his life is how, in an era when travel was rare, he managed to get around so much. We shouldn't really be surprised at this, however, for early Irish Christian monks were heavily inured with a travel bug, a tradition that continues to this day, for the Irish are still among the world's great travellers. Always eager to push back the frontiers of the possible, these monks journeyed to the most unimaginable of places at a time when travel was both difficult and dangerous. Their grasp of world geography might have been a trifle hazy, but they never allowed this become a hindrance. Unlike later pilgrims, they set off without a fixed destination in mind and were for the most part not concerned with returning to Ireland so, in this sense, it was impossible to become lost.

In the century following the arrival of St Patrick to Ireland, new monasteries sprang up, such as Clonard, Bangor, Clommacnoise and Clonfert. From these great ecclesiastical sites, monks, who referred to themselves as *peregrini*, spread out across Europe carrying the Christian message to a society where civil order had mostly broken down following the collapse of the Roman Empire. The simple narrative that is often proposed for this period, postulates Ireland as "the light in the west" returning the Christian faith to a grateful Europe when the continent had been plunged into dystopian darkness. As is often the case with such narratives, reality is far more complex. Journeying as undocumented migrants, the *peregrini* weren't always - as is still the case with such travellers - welcomed where they arrived.

One of the best-known *peregrinus* was Columbanus who, as a young man, joined the monastic settlement at Bangor. He left Ireland around 590AD to carry the Christian message to the Frankish and Lombard kingdoms. Founding a number of European monasteries, most notably Luxeuil in present-day France, he eventually fell foul of the local king and a jealous clergy who, understandably perhaps, had little use for the version of Celtic Christianity taught by an Irish immigrant. Ordered to leave the kingdom, he made his way south towards Europe's highest mountains. Crossing the Alps into what is today Italy, he established a monastery at Bobbio, which eventually became a major Benedictine foundation.

Among the other influential Irish saints of the period was St Killian, who went to Germany and did much to spread the gospel in the area around Wurzburg, only to become Ireland's first Christian martyr when he, unwisely perhaps, questioned the legality of the local king's marriage. A more fulsome and lasting welcome was extended to St Gall. He is still remembered fondly for bringing Christianity to Switzerland and establishing the city of St Gallen. Other successful Irish *peregrini*, included St Fursey who did missionary work in East Anglia and St Aiden who Christianised Northumbria.

An Irish missionary who today would probably be branded as a superstar apostle was the charismatic Saint Columba who was also known as Columbkille. After founding a string of monasteries across Ireland, most notably at Derry, he was ordered into exile following a dispute with a fellow holy man about the ownership of a copied book of psalms. Journeying to Scotland, he spread Christianity wherever he travelled and then went on to found the famous monastery on Iona Island.

The most renowned traveller of the period was, however, St Brendan, known as the "Navigator". During his life Brendan was a renowned wanderer and by far the most adventurous seafarer among the Irish Perigrini. Ordained by St Erc, he established monasteries at Ardfert, Co. Kerry and Clonfert, Co. Galway and reputedly Christianised the Dingle Peninsula by ousting pagan deity Crom Dubh from Mount Brandon and establishing instead a Christian oratory on the summit. A seafaring man to his fingertips, Brendan's first voyage took him to the Aran Islands, where he met with St Enda. It isn't surprising that he should have done this for Inis Mór is said to have the first Irish monastery and the place where many of the great Irish Saints came to be educated. He then fully justified the soubriquet "Navigator" by sailing to Scotland, Wales and finally the northern coast of France.

It is, however, for his legendary journey west from Ireland in search of the "Island Promised to the Saints", that we best know him. This was described in a very popular medieval page turner titled *Navigatio Sancti Brendan Abbatis* (*Voyage of Saint Brendan the Abbot*), that made him internationally renowned. Having been told of a legendary island to the west, where Christ was the light, he was apparently overwhelmed by curiosity. Building a wood-framed boat on the western slopes of Brandon, he covered it in oak-bark-tanned ox-hides, while smearing the joints with fat to keep them watertight. Brendan then fasted and celebrated mass on the mountain summit except, of course, it wasn't then called Brandon. It was known as Sliabh n-Aidche, for Brendan still had to make a name for himself. He did this by embarking on his famous voyage from Brandon Creek which lies directly in the mountain's shadow. *The Navigatio*, recounts how he sailed with 17 other monks on a voyage that lasted seven years and visited many faraway lands. It was filled with death defying adventures that, I guess, would have condemned most people living in the 21st Century to a bout of post-traumatic stress disorder.

Not so for Brendan. On one occasion, the saint thought he had discovered a new island. Happy with this, he went ashore with his companions to light a fire and cook a rare, hot meal. To his consternation, he then came to realise that the island was actually a giant sea monster when, not caring for the increase in temperature, the creature began to move away. A quick scamper back to the boat was then required, but such hair-raising adventures were apparently considered par for the course in the 6th Century.

Undeterred by this setback, Brendan and his companions went on to visit an island where sheep were the size of bulls. Later, the group sailed past a "smoking mountain from hell" and a huge column of crystal. Eventually, they made their way through a very foggy ocean to reach the Island Promised to the Saints, which was fertile and abounding with fruit trees. Here, an angel told them they had found their destination and must now return to Ireland.

When later explorers failed to find the mythical island of St Brendan, a new theory arose. It suggested that Brendan and his crew had actually sailed all the way across the Atlantic and that their final destination was the island that is today known as Newfoundland. In support of this argument, it was suggested that the island of sheep was the Faroes, the smoking mountain from hell was an Icelandic volcano, the column of crystal was an iceberg off the coast of Greenland and the foggy ocean was the Grand Banks area near Newfoundland, which is infamous for its persistent fog.

Nevertheless, the whole thing seemed a highly improbable story, since a currach built on a wooden frame covered by ox hide and waterproofed with animal fat, was the only boat available in Ireland during Brendan's time. It would be impossible, marine experts argued, for such a flimsy craft to make the trip from Ireland to America, since early boats were only able to sail before a following breeze and the prevailing winds ran in the opposite direction. Further, the ox hide skin of the boat would come apart with such long exposure to salt water and it would also be hugely difficult to navigate the great stretches of open ocean by the sun and stars in an area that is notoriously prone to cloud cover. Finally, the little leather currach would be smashed by Atlantic storms in what are some of the most dangerous waters in the world. In general, this is what most experts thought, and there the matter rested with the *Navigatio* treated as a charming but outlandish piece of medieval fiction.

Then over the horizon came one Tim Severin. A British explorer and historian, he was already noted for retracing the legendary historic journey of Venetian explorer Marco Polo and completing the length of the great Mississippi River. Convinced that the story of

St Brendan's voyage was based on fact, Severin built a replica of Brendan's currach. He used the techniques of the period and covered the boat with 49 tanned ox hides, which were sealed with wool grease before the boat was blessed by the Bishop of Kerry, Eamon Casey and christened *Brendan*.

Before a dubious crowd of local people who were only too aware of the dangers lying ahead for the fragile craft, Severin and four companions sailed forth from Brandon Creek, Co. Kerry, on May 17, 1976 and made a first stop at the Aran Islands, west of Galway city. So far so good, but then a severe gale almost did for them before they had even left Irish waters. Surviving, they landed in Co. Donegal to put an injured crewman ashore, before continuing to Scotland and the island of Iona. Here is located the renowned monastery that became a springboard for the conversion to Christianity of Northern England.

Then it was up the west coast of Scotland to the Outer Hebrides and onwards to traverse 200 miles of open ocean. Landing is always tricky for a totally sail-powered craft and when this presented serious difficulties, they were eventually towed ashore by a trawler to reach the Faroe Islands. Afterwards, a relatively uneventful crossing to Iceland followed, where they took the Brendan out of the water. She spent the winter in Reykjavik after an 8-week journey from Ireland.

On May 7, 1977 they resumed by setting course for Greenland. Reaching Iceland had been difficult but now they faced what would be the most isolated and challenging part of the expedition, where there would be no possibility of seeking shelter from a storm. Without an accompanying rescue craft, it is almost inconceivable that they could have been rescued from these freezing waters had the Brendan capsized. It was touch and go, for they were almost swamped by huge waves at one stage, but eventually they made it to the edge of the Arctic icepack and then began moving south. When the icepack threatened to trap them, they received another helpful tow from a Faroese fishing boat. Later, having being holed by ice, they were required to laboriously stitch a makeshift repair in the ox hide skin of the boat, while partly immersed in the sub-zero waters of the North Atlantic. On June 26 their 3,500-mile ocean journey was, nevertheless, completed, when the Brendan came ashore on Peckford Island, Newfoundland and thereby demonstrated that a voyage across the North Atlantic in a leather currach was possible.

It was an extraordinary feat of seamanship. With its medieval rigging, and no keel, the Brendan could not sail upwind and was also highly vulnerable to capsize. Nevertheless, the crew managed to bring her across the Atlantic against prevailing winds, which all proves, of course, St Brendan was the first European to reach North America.

Actually, it doesn't. The fact that a voyage across the North Atlantic in a leather currach was possible in the 20th Century doesn't actually mean it had happened in the 6th Century. Severin accepted this in his book *The Brendan Voyage* when he stated "in the final analysis the only conclusive proof that it had been done (St Brendan reaching America) will be if an authentic relic from an early Irish visit is found one day on North American soil". Admitting that this is unlikely, he added "If the early Irish did touch on North America, they would have left only the slightest fingerprint".

It must also be taken into account that Severin, despite the incredible difficulty of what he achieved, enjoyed several major advantages over Brendan. He was in radio contact with coastguards almost all the time, the crew wore modern waterproof clothing and possessed basic but still much superior navigational equipment when compared with what was available to Brendan and weren't faced with the challenge of a return journey. Most important of all was the fact that Severin knew where he was going and also carried accurate navigation charts. Comparing Brendan to Severin is like trying to equate today's climbers who ascend a highly sanitised Mount Everest with the original pioneers who had inferior equipment and didn't know what faced them. Finally, a helpful tow from a ship would not have been available to Brendan when things got tricky.

This is not, however, to exclude the possibility that St Brendan could not, in a period of seven years with many stops along the way, have succeeded in reaching North America. After all, Viking Leif Erickson, succeeded about 4 centuries later when sailing and navigational technology was much the same as it had been in Brendan's time.

Whether he counts as one of the world's greatest explorers or not, Brendan has an assured place in history as a hugely important Christian saint. He is by far the dominant spiritual brand on the Dingle Peninsula, with the otherwise almost ubiquitous St Patrick hardly getting a look in. And on a broader stage, he can also lay genuine claim to the title, most famous Irish born saint in history.

This fame has ensured that, as the story of the legendary apostle spread, pilgrims began journeying in veneration to the Dingle Peninsula, despite the fact that Brendan is actually buried at Clonfert, Co. Galway. Those coming overland headed west to what is now Cloghane and then ascended Brandon by a route known as the Pilgrim's Path to worship at the saint's oratory. But considering the location of Mount Brandon, it is clear many would have come using water borne transport. In the medieval period, Ventry Beach was the most convenient landing place for these pilgrims. They then followed a path known as the Saint's Road for the 18km walk to Mount Brandon.

For our visit to follow in the footsteps of these pilgrims and Brendan's heritage on the Dingle Peninsula, we'll now make a two-day excursion. First, we will traverse the wind-sculpted, Irish-speaking region beyond Mount Brandon and the Cosán na Naomh or Saints Road. It was along this route medieval pilgrims followed in the footsteps of Brendan to the mountain with which he is forever associated. Initially, we will find the path dallies along pleasant back roads and fuchsia-rich lanes with many echoes from the past in the form of ring forts, monastic sites and a ruined medieval castle, since the Dingle Peninsula is one of Ireland's most richly adorned landscapes for antiquities. Eventually, there is a delightful little boreen offering stunning views over the Three Sisters peninsula before we reach Gallarus Oratory, which I think you will consider the highlight of the Cosán.

An ancient place of worship, whose construction date has been lost to the mists of time, it is entirely built of unmortared stone with its apex roof giving the appearance of an upturned boat. Within the interior twilight is, however, where it comes most to life. Here, we will gaze in awe at the sublimely corbelled roof, which is the true glory of the place; it has not allowed even one drop of water to enter in over a thousand years.

On to Kilmalkedar Monastery, which was originally associated with St Brendan, but the later 12th Century church is almost certainly a hiberno-Romanesque relative of the sublime Cormac's Chapel in Cashel. This is a good place for us sit awhile in solitude and gaze out over the Atlantic Ocean while wondering if it was here Brendan - who has been traditionally associated with the place - first felt the urge to sail west to the Isle of the Blest. It is almost certain, you will then agree, that Kilmalkedar ticks all the right uncommercial, unpackaged boxes for definition as a genuine place apart.

Next, we will ascend Reenconnell Hill, on the summit of which persons unknown have carved a delightful rock spiral. For pilgrims past, this would have been a place of celebration, the first close up of the Promised Land with the ramparts of St Brendan's mountain filling the horizon. Then, it is on to our journey's end at Ballybrack which lies directly in the western shadow of Mount Brandon.

The next day, we head to the east side of the mountain and a small, scenic little car park at Faha. The sense of pilgrimage is reinforced as the waymarked route passes a grotto dedicated to Our Lady of the Mountains along with St Patrick and St Brendan. The traditional times of pilgrimage on Mount Brandon were May 16th, the feast day of St Brendan, and the last Sunday in July, which marked the ancient pagan festival of Lughnasa. When the pilgrimage was revived in 1868 as the Catholic Church became resurgent in Ireland, an estimated 20,000 people attended Mass on the summit. This was celebrated by David Moriarty, Bishop of Kerry, who was carried papal style to the summit in a sugán chair. The numbers may not be so big these days, but the ancient custom of pilgrimage to the summit continues with an organised ascent each year, which takes place in conjunction with the Féile Lughnasa in the village of Cloghane.

The well-worn path climbs steadily up a rather dull hill from the grotto but you must not be deterred by this for, as all great mountains do, Brandon reveals its secrets slowly. In good time, we will be given a first glimpse of the superb Coumaknock, which has been gouged out by ice and water, with its morosely bare rock and string of paternoster lakes stretched upwards like the beads of a gigantic rosary. Beyond Coumaknock some easy scrambling over user-friendly rocks is required to overcome some of the problems on the eroded path. Soon however, we will gain a ridge before continuing easily to the summit bearing the last skeletal remains of Brendan's oratory. Brandon is a famously mercurial mountain that is renowned for startling weather changes. If we chance upon the mountain in one of its good moods, however, we will feast upon arresting panoramas stretching from the Slievemish Mountains and then Carrauntoohil to the isolated Skellig Rocks and finally north along the Co. Clare coastline to the surreal outline of the far distant Aran Islands.

Afterwards, it is down the west side of Brandon where the green and grassy slopes stand in direct contrast to the great declivities and viserality of Coumaknock. On our descent, we will follow the convenient handrail provided by 14 Stations of the Cross and a solitary pagan standing stone. Below, on the left is the route of the ancient Cosán na Naomh which we walked yesterday from Ventry Beach while the staggeringly photogenic Blasket Islands will fill the horizon ahead.

By the time we arrive back at Ballybrack the termination point of yesterday's walk, it will have become abundantly clear that the area west of Dingle town is almost entirely cut off from the rest of Ireland by a chain of high, vertiginous mountains. Isolated and individualistic, the region has, throughout the course history, been defined not by the land of Ireland to which it is so tenuously attached but by the surrounding ocean and the robust seafaring tradition of its people. It would certainly have been the place to nurture seafaring men such as Brendan.

There is now just one more stop on our journey. This is at nearby Brandon Creek, where it is reputed Brendan departed on what would have been the first-ever trans-Atlantic voyage. Here is a simple but charming monument to the saint that adroitly captures the legend of Brendan: he is depicted sailing his tiny boat between two great slabs of sandstone. Down by the water's edge, we will find a marvellously evocative shoreline – a haven of shelter and serenity on an otherwise unforgiving coastline that has claimed many a victim including in 1588, the Santa Maria del la Rosa, which was one of the galleons of the Spanish Armada. Fed by the fall of a mountain stream from the Brandon Range, this steep-sided but placid creek seems to beckon the visitor towards the open ocean as it did for Brendan.

But this isn't on our agenda, for here is the place that marks the journey's end. It is also where we will have to accept that it is unlikely anyone will ever know for certain if Brendan succeeded in doing what the all-steel, 46,000-ton Titanic conspicuously failed to achieve: confronting the wild North Atlantic to reach the New World. Could he have reach North America while navigating by using the sun and stars on the minority of occasions these would be visible? If the answer is yes, his accomplishment far outshines - for sheer audacity and endurance - anything achieved by Christopher Columbus, Ronald Amundsen or even Neil Armstrong, and the appellation 'Navigator' will have been well and truly earned.

# CHAPTER 3

# The Winter Escape of the Ulster Princes

On reaching the Wicklow Gap, they were faced with an unpalatable truth. Not only had they escaped from Dublin Castle at the worst possible time of year, it was also during the late medieval period, which was one of the coldest weather eras in recent history. Having made it successfully this far, the trio of fugitives had quite literally run out of road. They had no option but to cross the high, trackless and snow-covered mountains south of the Gap in order to gain sanctuary. Even today, this is one of the most isolated parts of Wicklow that in poor conditions tests the competence of even the most well equipped and experienced hillwalker.

Surprising, as it may seem in this era of global warming, the late Middle Ages were also a time of climate change, but in the opposite direction. The 'Little Ice Age' is the term for a series of cold winters that occurred at this time that lasted for about a century beginning around 1570. Art O'Neill and Red Hugh O'Donnell, along with their guide, would now be exposed to its unrelenting icy blast. Their aim was to reach Ballinacor Castle, Glenmalure which was the redoubt of Fiach MacHugh O'Byrne. An ally of Hugh O'Neill, who had engineered their escape, O'Byrne had resoundingly defeated an incursion into his territory in 1580. But first they would have to trek the deep snows on Conavalla mountain while ill-clad and unprepared for such a challenge. Initially, they followed the secure guide of the Gleenremore Brook, but they were soon, however, confronted by the unforgiving northern ramparts of Conavalla. Struggling upwards, the princes eventually found they could go no further. Famished and exhausted, O'Neill and O'Donnell lay down in the snow and dispatched their guide to seek help from Glenmalure.

They wouldn't have known it then, but theirs was a time of transition in Irish history. At school, I remember the medieval history of this time being taught as a simple affair; it was a monochrome tale of black and white conflict between heroic Gael and perfidious Albion. The attempted British conquest of Ireland, we were told, ebbed and flowed for over four centuries in the face of heroic resistance. Finally, in the 16th Century, only two great Irish chieftains held out valiantly in a glorious attempt to protect the Catholic faith and Gaelic way of life in Ulster. These were Hugh O'Neill - known as the great O'Neill - and Red Hugh O'Donnell. O'Donnell had been treacherously kidnapped as a 15-year-old and borne away to imprisonment in Dublin Castle. Heroically, he escaped and then made his way back to Ulster to fight British oppression in Ireland. Along with his father-in-law and comrade in arms, Hugh O'Neill, he then defeated the armies of Queen Elizabeth I at battles such as the Yellow Ford and Curlew Pass.

Ultimate victory was almost guaranteed when in September 1600 a military expedition from Spain, which was then the principal bulwark against the Protestant Reformation, set out for Ireland. The idea was to link with the northern rebel forces and finally drive the English out of Ireland. Irish history was, however, one long succession of hard luck stories, or so we were told. Driven ashore by storms, the Spanish landed, not in Ulster, but on the south coast of Ireland with almost 4000 soldiers decanting to the town of Kinsale, where they immediately came under siege from the English army. The Ulster chiefs were then forced to march their armies hundreds of miles to relieve them in what, as Irish ill-luck would have it, was one of the coldest winters in living memory. It is recounted in the

Annals of the Four Masters that along the way, O'Donnell emphasised his Catholicism, by pausing to pray for success before the relic
of the true cross in Holy Cross Abbey.

These prayers were not, however, answered. Arriving tired and
in no condition to fight, the armies of O'Neill and O'Donnell were
quickly defeated by the English. Following the Battle of Kinsale, the
sadly melancholic Flight of the Earls occurred. O'Neill and O'Donnell
abandoned their ancestral homeland and poignantly fled to mainland Europe; this ended forever the Gaelic way of life in Ireland.

But history isn't monochrome or easily explained by simple
narratives; more often it is a rich and complex tapestry that defies
simple explanation. And so, something struck me forcibly some time
ago about The Flight of the Earls! Why an English crown title? Surely
it should have been The Flight of the Chieftains. Clearly, there was
something going on here, so I decided to start digging for the facts
of Irish 16th Century history and this is the story that I uncovered.

Red Hugh O'Donnell was born in 1572, into one of the most
renowned Irish clans during a time when the power of these great
families was being threatened by the Tudor reconquest of Ireland.
This reconquest began when England's Henry VIII was declared King
of Ireland in 1542, with the aim of reclaiming Irish territories that had
been lost during the previous centuries and thus to prevent these areas
falling into the hands of hostile powers. The great Anglo-Norman families such as the Fitzgeralds and Butlers already held English aristo-
cratic titles and were seen as subject to the English king. Now however,
Gaelic lords were also required to surrender their lands, chieftainships
and autonomy in return for English earldoms and allowing succession of the first-born, legitimate son. The recent execution of Silken
Thomas, the Earl of Kildare and five of his uncles, who had recently
rebelled against English rule showed that this time Henry meant business. Soon after, Red Hugh's grandfather, Manus O'Donnell, along
with most other Gaelic chieftains, saw it in his interest to visit London

and submit himself and his territories to Henry VIII. In return, he was regranted his lands and became Earl of Tyrconnell.

This appeared to solve the frequent feuds over succession among O'Donnell clan members, but in the double-dealing world of Tudor politics nothing was ever simple. All the inherent dilemmas and complications of colonial rule, which have since become starkly apparent throughout the intervening centuries in Ireland, were now manifesting themselves in Ulster. In today's world, the O'Donnell's would probably be classed as a dysfunctional family with self-destructive tendencies and abnormally high levels of inter-familial jealously that required the urgent intervention of a family therapist. These were medieval times, however, and the rulers of Tyrconnell just behaved as everyone else did - at all costs they sought to obtain and then hold onto power.

Tensions over succession within the clan saw Manus deposed by his son Calvagh. When Calvagh died, his half-brother Hugh was inaugurated. Red Hugh was then born to Hugh and his Scottish born second wife, Finola McDonnell, whose influential father held the title Lord of the Isles. To Finola's dismay, it was however, Red Hugh's elder half-brother, Donnell who, with English support, became the heir-apparent to the Earldom of Tyrconnell.

It is sometimes said that in the medieval period there were no teenage years – young people plunged directly from childhood to the pressures of adult responsibility. And so, it came to pass that, at the age of 15, the young Red Hugh was betrothed to Rose O'Neill, daughter of Hugh O'Neill, the Earl of Tyrone. This was, of course, at a time when the human race had still to invent the notion of romantic love; early marriage was then seen as both necessary and functional for the survival of the clan. In this case, the idea here was to cement a powerful alliance between the O'Neill and O'Donnell clans, who had long been sworn enemies, but would now join to oppose English interference in Ulster.

This coming together of the two most powerful Gaelic families in Ulster did not sit well in Dublin. Soon after, Red Hugh was tricked into boarding what he thought was a Spanish wine-trading vessel that had sailed into Rathmullan Harbour, in what is now Co. Donegal. In reality, it was an English ship that had been sent by Sir John Perrot, Queen Elizabeth's Lord Deputy of Ireland. Borne away from his betrothed, Red Hugh was held as a hostage in the Birmingham Tower of Dublin Castle as insurance against the O'Donnell's misbehaving themselves. Hostage taking was not unusual in the medieval period, but hostages were generally well treated. O'Donnell was not, however, and this led to a lasting resentment against the English crown that would colour his later actions.

Apparently not a woman to let grass grow beneath her feet, Red Hugh's formidable mother, Finola, now took action. Known locally as the Iníon Dubh or the black daughter, she became the powerhouse behind the throne as her husband aged and was soon displaying credentials as the ultimate step-mother from hell. In the Orwellian world of Tudor politics, just about anything was acceptable in the pursuit of power; Finola imported mercenary soldiers from her native Scotland and with their help defeated and killed her stepson, Donnell, at the Battle of Doire Leathan in 1590. Assassinating one's way to power was not at all uncommon in Tudor times and Red Hugh was now the undisputed heir to the Earldom of Tyrconnell. There was one problem, however: he remained a prisoner, held at the pleasure of the English Lord Deputy of Ireland in Dublin Castle.

With the help of his future father-in-law Hugh O'Neill, the 2nd Earl of Tyrone, Red Hugh made a bid for freedom on the night of January 6, 1592. Accompanied by brothers Art and Henry McShane O'Neill – who were cousins of Hugh O'Neill – Red Hugh O'Donnell scrambled down a lavatory chute using an improvised rope. At this point Art injured his foot in a fall, which was a bad omen for the start of a 50km trek. Crossing the River Dodder, they did, however, manage to make their way to freedom beyond the walls of what was then a tiny city. Theirs would be the first and only successful prisoner escape that has ever been recorded from Dublin Castle.

With one brave dash the princes were free, but far from safe. The plan was that horses would be provided to facilitate their escape, but these failed to materialise so they were obliged to continue on foot. Under the guidance of Turlough O'Hagen, who had been sent by Hugh O'Neill, to facilitate the escape, they first headed southwest through the present suburbs of Harold's Cross, Kimmage, Templeogue, Firhouse and Ballyboden and were soon outside the area of Ireland where direct English rule applied. Someplace along the way, Henry became detached from the others and made his own way back to Ulster. Tradition holds, Art and Red Hugh continued through the western foothills of the Wicklow Mountains, thus avoiding the wildest and most unforgiving terrain that lies around the present Sally Gap.

Exactly how they journeyed after this is impossible to say. They could have followed the route of the modern-day Art O'Neill Challenge over Black Hill and through Billy Byrne's Gap to gain the Wicklow Gap. An alternative - which is not an option today because of the flooding of the area to create the Pollaphuca reservoir - would have been to traverse the low-level King's River Valley lying further west. Considering the weather conditions of the time, this would appear to have been the more attractive option.

By whatever means they successfully managed to reach the Wicklow Gap, which, considering the prevailing conditions, was in itself a considerable achievement. According to tradition, they then headed south by the Glenreemore Valley, but on the unforgiving slopes of Conavalla Mountain, found it impossible to go further. The services of a mountain rescue team were urgently required, but none existed in medieval Ireland. Instead, their guide was dispatched to Ballinacor Castle, Glenmalure to seek help.

Fiach MacHugh O'Byrne responded by sending some of his men with food and beer but when they reached the Ulster princes, both were unconscious. Art never regained consciousness and his remains now repose somewhere amid the lonesome blanket bogs of the Wicklow uplands. In the 20th Century, a cross was positioned on the mountainside above the location where he is, by tradition, reputed to have passed away. O'Donnell came around enough, however, to intake some food and then recovered sufficiently to make it down to the safety of Glenmalure. Unsurprisingly, it took him a considerable period to recover from his ordeal, by which time he had had his big toes amputated due to the effects of frostbite.

While the general consensus holds that the Ulster Princes followed a somewhat westerly route through the Wicklow Mountains, it is worth mentioning here that in the *Journal of the Irish Mountaineering and Exploration Historical Society 2005*, Tomás Ó Cuinn recounts a strong tradition he encountered in Glenmalure. It stated that Art O'Neill died not at the head of Glenreemore but at Dromgoff, which lies between Glendalough and Glenmalure. If true, this would suggest the route followed by the fugitives commenced further east in the Wicklow Gap than had previously been believed, but this would not necessarily have been any easier to follow. Certainly, Drumgoff would have made a shorter and somewhat less demanding hike for Turlough O'Hagan when going to Ballincor to seek help. On the other hand, the annals state that Art passed away beneath a high cliff, which suggests Glenreemore. It is, however, such fascinating contradictions that makes the study of history so intriguing.

What is certain is that O'Donnell was led across high and trackless mountains to reach the safety of Glenmalure, where he was eventually restored to health. Afterwards, he journeyed back to Ulster and after many nerve-wracking encounters along the way, arrived back to Tyrconnell. Here, at the age of just 20, he stood on the Rock of Doone, (the traditional inauguration stone for O'Donnell chiefs) and was proclaimed as The O'Donnell, Prince of Tyrconnell. Unsurprisingly, perhaps he had, to use modern parlance, been radicalised by his prison experiences. Now an implacable enemy of English rule in Ireland, O'Donnell nursed a deeply felt sense of grievance which made him a most dangerous adversary.

Meanwhile, his father-in-law, Hugh O'Neill - who had until recently co-operated with English rule and indeed once played the role of Queen Elizabeth's chief enforcer in Ireland - had a change of heart. Although never an exemplary Catholic, O'Neill now saw it in his interests to ally himself with the Catholic Counter-Reformation, which was aimed at halting the advance of Protestantism in all parts of Europe. In modern management speak this would probably be referred to as harvesting synergies, but from O'Neill's point of view it simply gave him a more powerful hand to play. Soon he renounced the Earldom of Tyrone, and reverted to the ancient Gaelic title of The O'Neill and become the leading exponent for Catholicism in Ireland.

This snub to the English monarchy immediately had him on a collision course with crown forces in Ireland, for there was no greater offence in the Elizabethan world than that of treason against the monarch. Having now crossed his Irish Rubicon, O'Neill immediately formed an alliance with O'Donnell that was aimed at eliminating English rule from Ireland.

Initially, what later became known as the Nine Years War went well for the Ulster rebels, who had now formed an unshakeable alliance. With logistical support from the Catholic monarch, Philip III of Spain, and fighting a defensive campaign in ideal terrain for such tactics, the northern chiefs repulsed, with remarkable tenacity, many attempts to march into their territories. Nevertheless, the conquest of Ireland was slowly moving under Queen Elizabeth from an aspiration to an ongoing operation. The English managed to gain a foothold in Ulster with a seaborne landing at Derry, which conveniently bypassed the necklace of mountains, lakes and bogs that guard the province to the south. Now under pressure, O'Neill and O'Donnell made a joint appeal for direct military intervention in Ireland from Philip III. Had they been able to see into the future, the Ulster chiefs would have recognized the omens were not good. Over the centuries, Ireland has, at various times, sought Scottish, Spanish, French, American and German help to repulse the British occupation of the island - but all to no avail. In fact, liberation only came after a War of Independence that was successful without any outside intervention.

When the smaller than expected Spanish army did eventually arrive to Kinsale, Co. Cork, Lord Mountjoy, the English Lord Deputy in Ireland, laid siege to them with 7,000 men. O'Neill and O'Donnell then marched south to trap Mountjoy's army between the Irish and the Spanish.

It is easy to be critical of the Ulster chiefs for leaving the security of their northern redoubt and undertaking the long, perilous march south to Kinsale, rather than, perhaps, attacking the lightly defended Dublin. But, as with all history, later generations know what was going to happen next – O'Neill and O'Donnell didn't. With the English suffering severely from malnutrition and disease at Kinsale, the signs would have seemed favorable for a Spanish/Irish victory and the end of English rule in Ireland.

Having crossed over the western end of the Slieve Bloom Mountains, they then avoided a possible ambush near Cashel by marching under the cover of darkness over the Slieve Felim Mountains. Eventually, the Ulster chiefs made it to Kinsale. Here, on exposed ground, they were far out of their comfort zone which lay with defensive actions amid the lakes, bogs and mountains ringing Ulster. Ever cautious, O'Neill wished to follow the sensible course of action by starving the English into submission, but the more bellicose O'Donnell argued for an attack on Mountjoy's forces. Surprised by a sudden counter attack, as they prepared an assault on the English lines, the Irish chieftains were routed and retreated forlornly to Ulster, while the Spanish surrendered and were returned home.

Unable perhaps, to cope with the magnitude of the defeat, O'Donnell left Ireland almost immediately and sailed to Corunna in Galicia, Spain with the promise to his supporters that he would return to Ireland with a large army. This was not to be the case, however; he would never return to his the native Tyrconnell.

On arrival in Spain, he was given an effusive welcome from the Governor of Galicia, which must have been a considerable boost to his sagging confidence. He then followed in the footsteps of many earlier Irish pilgrims on the penitential route to Santiago de Compostela that is now known as the Celtic Camino. Here, he was made an honoured guest of the Archbishop and stayed in the episcopal palace. No doubt visualizing a glorious return to Ireland, Red Hugh travelled on to the Spanish royal court at Valladolid to ask further help from Philip III of Spain, who apparently committed himself to a second invasion of Ireland. Time went by, however, and O'Donnell did not receive any favourable response from Philip who had become short of money and after recent failures was, perhaps, wary of further expensive expeditions against the English.

Impatient for action as ever, he set out again for Valladolid to try a second time at persuading Philip, but died unexpectedly enroute at Simincas Castle on September 10, 1602. Two explanations have been put forward for his untimely demise at the age of 30: one being he was poisoned by an English spy; the other was that he died of a parasite infection.

When Hugh O'Neill learned of O'Donnell's death, he realised that Spanish aid would not be forthcoming and that his cause was lost. In the same month as O'Donnell's death, the traditional inauguration stone of the O'Neill Chieftains at Tullavogue, Co. Tyrone was, in a hugely symbolic act, smashed by English forces. Afterwards, O'Neill felt obliged to sign the Treaty of Mellifont in 1603 where he would continue as Earl of Tyrone but as a vassal of the English crown. The Nine Years War had finally come to an end and with it the ancient Gaelic order of clan kinship in Ireland.

According to the Annals of the Four Masters, Red Hugh was afforded a royal funeral in Spain. "His body was conveyed to the king's palace at Valladolid in a four-wheeled hearse, surrounded by countless numbers of the king's state officers, council, and guards, with luminous torches and bright flambeaux of beautiful wax-light burning on each side of him." Afterwards, he was buried in the Franciscan monastery at Valladolid, but no trace of his grave now remains. He was then succeeded by his younger brother Rory as Earl of Tyrconnell.

Whatever the cause of his untimely demise, Red Hugh's was certainly a very full life. Lucky to survive into manhood, he was impulsive, hot-headed and also ruthless by our 21st Century standards. Yet, with his more considered father-in-law, he came the closest that there has ever been to completely excluding the English crown from the entire island of Ireland.

Showing little of the deep sense of Irishness that motivated later revolutionaries such as Charles Kickham, Tom Barry and Liam Lynch, he appears to have been driven more by an understandable anti-Englishness than any desire to create an independent Irish nation. Paradoxically, he has, along with Hugh O'Neill, remained a great a hero in Ireland by appearing to embody the very essence of what it is to be Irish, while in his lifetime showing little to suggest he understood or indeed cared about this concept. Like most rulers in the Tudor period, what O'Donnell did care about was acquiring and holding power and, in his particular case, protecting the Gaelic way of life in Ulster. In this he failed.

Fearing arrest, his father-in-law, Hugh O'Neill, and brother Rory bowed to the inevitable in 1607 and sailed out of Lough Swilly in what has since become known as the Flight of the Earls. For the first time, England had uncontested control of every part of Ireland. The ensuing plantation of Ulster meant that, within a short time, the most staunchly Gaelic of the Irish provinces would be transformed into the most British and most divided.

We take from history what we need and O'Donnell's memory is, undoubtedly, destined to live on. It is preserved by a large statue in his native Donegal while a walking route in Upperchurch, Co. Tipperary (The Red Hugh Loop) recalls part of the route he is reputed to have taken on his march to Kinsale. Finally, he is commemorated annually as part of the Art O'Neill challenge. This, continually oversubscribed event, takes place each year in January. It is then that 200 ultra-runners and walkers plunge out in darkness to a wintry Wicklow. They then follow 55km in the footsteps of Art and Hugh on the, even today, long and exhausting traverse from Dublin Castle to Glenmalure.

CHAPTER 4

# The East Munster Rapparees

"You go to bed so and I'll watch out for you. I hope you don't have nightmares after eating that cheese," said Tomás.

Eamon an Chnoic then falls asleep, while Tomás picks up an axe.

"Ná buail mé. Have mercy for heaven's sake. What – O Tomás. I had the most awful nightmare. I thought someone was creeping up behind me with an axe. I suppose I saw that axe of yours in the corner before I fell asleep," said Eamon.

"I only keep that ould axe for splitting firewood. As a matter of fact, now that you've reminded me, I might sharpen it up and split a few while I am looking out for you. I hope it won't wake you."

"Not at all, go ahead. I'm really very tired. I doubt if anything could wake me,"

Tomás then edges the axe, while Eamon falls asleep

"Nooo. O my God, I had the same nightmare again."

"Calm down, Eamon, calm down. Relax. All this running around from Maude [Robert Maude, High Sherriff of Tipperary] has affected your nerves and you haven't been eating properly either. Take some of this warm milk."

"Thanks so. Maybe it will be third time lucky."

"Third time lucky usually works for me."

"Right so and good night."

Eamon falls asleep. Tomás picks up the axe.

*– Extracted from the play, Eamon an Chnoic,*

*by Billy Clancy, Upperchurch*

\* \* \*

In the century and a half previous to the time depicted by this play, the land of Ireland moved from 100% Catholic owned to less than 5% in such ownership. This had involved the forced dispossession of Catholic landowners on an extravagant scale and created a deep and lasting pit of resentment. It was a land-grab, of course, but then much of the land was taken from Anglo-Norman families, who had earlier grabbed this land during the Norman Conquest, which all goes to prove that historic blame is always difficult to allocate.

The consequence was the gentrification of the Irish countryside, with wealthy English settlers arriving to build palatial mansions on great estates that survive to this day. But this new ruling class lacked legitimacy among ordinary people, many of whom were drawn from the ranks of the evicted from long held landholdings. Necessary journeys were, at this time, made either on horseback or by carriage and as trade increased there were growing numbers of well-to-do people undertaking these trips. Such travellers were extremely vulnerable to attack, since there was no organised police force in Ireland prior to the 19th Century. While the punishments for even petty theft were draconian, there was limited capacity for the British appointed high sheriffs in each county to enforce these laws among a truculent and uncooperative populace.

In such a fertile ground for lawlessness, every area of Ireland had its highwaymen and outlaws who lived off rich pickings. Some were undoubtedly scoundrels, who took advantage of the state of lawlessness that existed in much of the Irish countryside at the time. Others were genuinely drawn from the ranks of the dispossessed or were former Jacobite soldiers who continued to resist the injustices laid upon the Catholic community after the defeat of James II, with their role once succinctly described as afflicting the comfortable and comforting the afflicted.

In either case, the impoverished majority had little to fear from their activities and so these untamed individuals easily morphed into folk heroes that were much admired for their boldness and daring. Many were, after their deaths, elevated to a cult status as lovable, but resolutely non-conformist, rogues. This was at a time when ordinary people felt entirely oppressed and possessed little in the way of other anti-establishment role models.

One of the most famous was James Freney, who was born near Inistioge, Co. Kilkenny and became known as "Freney the Robber". He terrorised areas around the South Kilkenny hills for a period of 5 years but was reputedly generous with his takings towards the Catholic poor. Carrying a price on his head, he eventually surrendered when the hangman's noose threatened and, unusually for a rapparee, was pardoned. Subsequently, he brazenly wrote a best-selling autobiography titled rather euphemistically, *The Life and Adventures of Mr James Freney*.

Count Redmond O'Hanlon, like many other Irish outlaws, came from noble Catholic stock in Ulster. Renowned as a rapparee and folk hero in the upland areas around Slieve Gullion, Co. Armagh, he allegedly robbed English settlers and gave to the native Irish, who had recently been disinherited by the Ulster Plantation. With a price on his head, he was, according to local tradition, murdered in his sleep by a kinsman. O'Hanlon's popularity was later immortalised in poems and ballads which have survived up to the present. Similarly, eulogised was the Limerick rapparee, Michael "Galloping" Hogan, who led Patrick Sarsfield to destroy the Williamite siege guns at Ballyneety, Co. Limerick. He departed for Europe soon after the defeat of King James and went on to have a successful military career on the continent.

James Maclaine was a Monaghan born highwayman who, unusually for the time, hailed from a well-to-do Presbyterian family. Fitting neatly into the category of unprincipled scoundrel, he became known as the "Gentleman Highwayman" because of his polite behaviour during robberies, which has me imagining "Sorry to bother, but would you mind awfully handing over all your jewellery, madame?" Moving to London, having squandered his inheritance, he famously robbed future British Prime Minister Horace Walpole before eventually being hanged for his crimes at Tyburn.

In East Munster, two outlaws from this period have, however, entered popular folklore to an extent that has eclipsed almost all others. This was perhaps because of an uncanny parallel between their life stories, which appear to contain all the necessary pre-requisites for myth-building. In the best rapparee tradition, outlaws William Crotty and Eamon an Chnoic are both alleged to have robbed the rich but only to help the poor, although they may have retained some cash to cover expenses. Having been forced to become outlaws by reason of dispossession, each was active during the 18th Century in East Munster. This was at a time when the Catholic majority in Ireland was at its most downtrodden and it is perhaps unsurprising that both quickly morphed into role models for resistance to tyranny. When the situation became uncomfortably tricky, each took refuge in a secluded mountain cave. Ruthless and cunning when the situation required, they were, nevertheless, much admired and mythologised by the ordinary people. Using local knowledge of their native hill country they evaded capture for many years before each being betrayed by an accomplice. In the end both outlaws came to a sticky end; they were decapitated as an example to those who would usurp the rule of English law in Ireland. Following their deaths, rumours abounded of a hoard of hidden gold they had left behind that awaited a lucky finder. No finder ever came forward, but the outlaws, nevertheless, continue to be lauded in song and story as folk heroes by the people of the East Munster uplands. Each outlaw has had a play written in his honour, while Eamon an Chnoic is also commemorated by a very popular loop through the hill country above Upperchurch village.

One was described thus in a contemporary account, "Erect as a spear shaft, slightly above middle height and with the black piercing eyes of an eagle, a suntanned face eminent and beautiful in its proportions, a mass of shining black hair". This was Edmund O'Ryan, (Eamon an Chnoic) who was born during the 1660s into a relatively prosperous Catholic family in the townland of Archseanbó in the parish of Upperchurch, Co. Tipperary. His ancestors were extensive landowners, whose lands were confiscated during the Munster plantation a century earlier with his family reduced to tenants on their own land. In common with many others from Catholic families at the time, he was sent to the Irish College at Louvain, within what is now Belgium, to study for the priesthood. Having returned home for a period, he is reputed to have witnessed a bailiff who was seizing a cow from an impoverished widow in lieu of rent. Eamon took strong exception to this and killed the bailiff. This act of defiance undoubtedly raised his status with the local community but created certain personal difficulties. He now had blood on his hands so he could no longer go forward for holy orders and there was soon a price on his head. Forced to go on the run in order to avoid the hangman's noose, he took refuge in the relatively untamed Slieve Felim Hills of Co. Tipperary.

When King James II arrived in Ireland in 1689, it is easy to see why Eamon would have made common cause with the Jacobites since they appeared to promise religious freedom and restoration of confiscated Catholic land. He fought at the Battle of the Boyne, which was, by a country mile, the most significant combat ever entered into on Irish soil. Caught in a pincer movement, the Jacobite army was forced to retreat, with James reputedly much to the fore in this rapid withdrawal. Two days later King William of Orange took Dublin and the Protestant ascendancy was assured.

Eamon subsequently saw action at the Battle of Aughrim and the Siege of Limerick, as the Jacobites tried to regroup in Connaught, but it was all to no avail. After the war ended, the Irish leader Patrick Sarsfield and most of his soldiers went to fight on the continent. Surprisingly, Eamon did not accompany them; a romantic involvement was suggested locally as the reason. Instead, he returned to the hill country and lived as an outlaw, continually attacking and robbing English planters in the North Tipperary area.

The other famous outlaw of East Munster was William Crotty. He was born at Russellstown on the western edge of the Comeragh Mountains, the son of a poor farmer who was evicted from his holding. Active during the early part of the 18th Century he was, unlike Eamon an Chnoic and Redmond O Hanlon, not of genteel extraction and does not appear to have become an outlaw as part of an ideological opposition to English rule in Ireland. Details about him are a trifle hazy, but he seems to have become a rapparee simply because few other options presented themselves to the dispossessed.

If that is the case it was, initially at least, a successful choice. He became the leader of a gang of highwaymen who, according to local tradition, stole from the rich to give to the poor, much in the same manner as Robin Hood. With an unmatched knowledge of the Comeragh Mountains he was adept at giving his pursuers the slip by hiding in a remote cave in his high mountain fastness, which, it was reputed, could only be accessed by use of a rope.

Unable to capture him, the British authorities soon resorted to bribing his close associate David Norris. According to legend, Norris, having tipped off the authorities of his whereabouts, plied Crotty with whiskey to make him sleepy, before wetting Crotty's gunpowder and stealing his dagger. When soldiers arrived, Crotty was easy meat: inebriated and defenceless. He was put on trial at Ballybricken in Waterford City and found guilty. After being hanged, his head was cut off and was left on display outside the county jail as a warning to other outlaws. Then, in a final melodramatic denouement, his wife is reputed to have jumped to her death from the rocks above his hideout.

Setting out to retrace the footsteps of Crotty from Coolnalingady, Co. Waterford, I followed a farm track uphill. Local legend holds that Crotty's golden hoard still awaits a lucky finder somewhere amid the Comeragh fastness. To explore what is now called the Crotty Country, I struck out across open mountainside towards a pair of great beckoning pinnacles. Expansive views over the magnificently serene Crotty's Lake now helped to grease the wheels of my ascent until I reached the spectacular viewing point at Crotty's Rock where the outlaw is reputed to have kept watch for hostile forces. In such an eventuality, plan B was a retreat to a claustrophobic cave located on the opposite side of the lake.

Contouring south, I crossed the busy little stream of Iske Sullas, which drops away in cascades that have carved deeply attractive gorges into the underlying bedrock. Next stop is the great cliff that overlooks Coumshingaun, the show-pony for glaciated coums on these islands. From here the eye is immediately drawn to a substantial rockfall nearby the northwest corner of the lake. The fallen boulders have created a cave system, where reputedly Crotty found a hiding place for his horses, all of which had been shod in reverse to confuse pursuing redcoats.

North-westwards now across a featureless plateau to gain the cliffs guarding the Comeraghs' most secluded and least visited coum. Below are three enchanting little lakes, while beyond the glacial moraines the countryside rolls away picturesquely towards Curraheen. Here, it is suggested by some, Crotty's hoard lies secreted beneath an isolated rock and that on occasion his ghost is to be seen searching on horseback for this lost treasure.

Then, it is back to Crotty's Lake for exploration of the outlaw's hideout. When many years ago I first went looking for Crotty's Cave, its inaccessibility was emphasised by the fact that I failed to find it on my initial attempt. Availing of local knowledge, I did subsequently uncover its entrance in a small crag just above the lake. Immediately obvious was the fact that the cave is accessible without a rope. Nevertheless, it was clear all the advantages lay with the defender. The entrance requires an upward scramble through a narrow horizontal fissure where an attacker would be extremely vulnerable to assault from above. Then, it was a tight squeeze down a passage before the cave turns sharply to reach a ledge, which would have made a rough sleeping place for the outlaw.

While the cave is undoubtedly well concealed, it immediately struck me how tough and unglamorous the life of an 18th Century outlaw would have been. The idea that the cave would have been a hideout for Crotty had, however, a ring of truth; desperate measures would have been necessary to avoid the hangman's noose, and here appeared to be the best possible sanctuary. I also noticed there was a fissure in the cave roof which would have allowed escape upwards in a dire emergency. Hiding in this dark, damp cave would clearly have made for a tough, uncomfortable existence which would hardly have been compensated for by the possession of a golden hoard.

Eamon an Chnoic was also betrayed by a fellow outlaw. Reuben Lee was a soldier in Cromwell's army, who remained behind and joined the Irish rapparees. Local folklore holds that in contrast to Eamon, who divided it amongst the poor, Reuben kept the money he stole. Having amassed his fortune, he offered to hand Eamon over to the British authorities in return for his own pardon. A deal was agreed and Reuben arranged to invite Eamon to his house on a certain date when the redcoats would swoop to arrest him.

Fortunately for Eamon, his facility with the Irish language ensured the plan went awry. A local man named Ryan became suspicious of Lee after he spotted redcoats in the vicinity. He went to Lee's house and informed Eamon of the danger through the medium of Irish, which Lee did not speak. The outlaw was immediately on his guard and kept a close eye through the window. When he saw British soldiers stealthily approaching, he shot Lee and then made a hasty escape. Reuben's remains were then buried in Upperchurch cemetery but when the locals discovered how he had betrayed their hero, they disinterred the body and flung it into a river.

One advantage that Eamon an Chnoic had over Crotty was an education. It would seem probable that he is the likely author of the ballad written in Gaelic titled Eamon an Chnoic with the well-known opening line "Cé hé sin amuigh, a bhuil faobhar ar a guth". It describes the life of a 17th Century outlaw in the type of stark, unromanticised detail that would suggest it was written by an educated person, most likely with actual experience of being on the run.

In one poignant verse, the outlaw describes his situation thus:

> I am a long time outside in snow and in frost never daring to approach anyone, my fallow (fields) unsown, my plough team untied, I am without them and any friends.

Local tradition holds that Eamon was eventually murdered in the home of Tomás Bán Dwyer near Foilaclug, which lies between the villages of Cappawhite and Hollyford. It seems this individual gave refuge to the outlaw, at that time in 1724, when he believed the outlaw had a price of £300 on his head. Worth about €60,000 in today's money, this was a considerable temptation among an impoverished peasantry. A reward for the head of an outlaw was then seen as the most effective way of neutralizing them in what was generally a lawless society.

As Eamon slept, Tomás, unable to resist temptation, decapitated him with an axe. He then placed the head in a sack and headed for Cashel where he hoped to reap the reward from the local High Sherriff, Robert Maude. What he did not know was that Eamon was highly respected for his chivalry and had just recently been pardoned and granted a safe passage abroad. No reward would now be paid for his killing. According to popular lore, his head was then returned to the Slieve Felim area and buried at Curraheen near Hollyford, while his torso was interred by local people in a graveyard at Doon, Co. Limerick.

In the 18th Century footsteps of Eamon an Chnoic, I headed into the Slieve Felim country in search of the cave which was reputedly his hideout. Eventually, I found it amid the old red sandstone hills lying to the south of Hollyford. It is certainly in a secluded location just above a stream, but if Crotty's could be judged a four-star cave for an outlaw, this is certainly in the one-star category. Small and wet, it is an abode to use only in the direst of circumstances, although such was probably the case for much of Eamon's life. Standing there at the tiny cave, it occurred to me that anti-authoritarian role models are an essential coping mechanism in times when ordinary people feel oppressed by external forces.

Every community tends to recreate and fine-tune its history through the process of storytelling. It is, perhaps, unsurprising then, that after their deaths, William Crotty and Eamon an Chnoic morphed into quixotic 18th Century heroes. Their moral legitimacy arose from highly embroidered tales of a struggle against a ruling class that regarded then as just common criminals. Never of more significant than a nuisance for British rulers in Ireland, they were, nevertheless, lauded by the common people for they were seen as fearlessly refusing to be ruled by an oppressor and working instead to subvert the authority of an illegitimate state. And as perhaps Ireland's first socialists, they had, in the public mind, striven to ensure a fairer distribution of wealth within a grossly unequal society.

So, is it possible that the highly embellished tales of the East Munster rapparees could still hold a strong element of truth? To try and answer this question, I made the short journey to nearby Curraheen. Here, a substantial monument has been raised to Eamon's memory. It is in the farmyard of Dermot Ryan, who proves a mine of information about the outlaw.

According to Mr Ryan, the place where Eamon was reputed to have been buried was marked on the original 19th Century ordnance survey map. In 1963 Matthew Ryan – a commander in the US navy and descendant of Eamon - decided to put a monument at this location. When the earth was being excavated for the building of the monument at Currraheen, workmen came across a neatly constructed stone cavity containing a skull without a body attached to it.

# CHAPTER 5

# Vanquished by a New Road

Their situation seemed hopeless. Surrounded, in a cottage lying beneath Kaedeen Mountain, Co. Wicklow, the prospects of escape appeared bleak. Earlier, Michael Dwyer – a veteran of the 1798 Rebellion and continuing thorn in the side for British rule in Ireland – had, with 12 companions, taken shelter from a blizzard in the winter of 1799. They were in three adjacent cottages, which were located in an isolated townland known as Derrynamuck in the Glen of Imaal. The British authorities became aware of their presence and before the rebels had time to flee, they were encircled by 100 redcoats from the Glengarry Regiment who were based in nearby Hackettstown. Dwyer requested the families living in the cottages be allowed safe passage through the line of soldiers, as they had not willingly sheltered the outlaws, and the redcoats agreed.

Soon after, the men in the other two cottages surrendered, leaving Dwyer and three companions - including Sam McAllister from Antrim - in the remaining cottage, which then refused to surrender. The cottage was set ablaze and a fierce gunfight ensued, during which McAllister was seriously wounded. Deciding he could not escape; the Antrim man offered to open the door and thus draw a volley of musket fire. Since repeating rifles had not been invented at that time, there would then be a pause while the soldiers reloaded; this would allow a brief chance for escape.

Flinging open the door of the cottage and deliberately stepping into the line of fire, McAllister was immediately gunned down, but acting on his comrade's plan, Dwyer used the lull in the firing to make a dash for freedom. Running barefoot through the snow, a lucky slip in the ice caused a volley of musket balls to pass harmlessly over his head. By wading the swollen River Slaney, he alone escaped the cottage as the redcoats, attired in full military regalia, were unable to follow. A fortunate escape undoubtedly, but also the moment that would forever copper fasten Michael Dwyer's heroic place in Irish history.

Born during 1772 in the Glen of Imaal, Co. Wicklow, Dwyer was the eldest of seven children raised by John and his wife Mary (*née* Byrne). His father was a poor tenant farmer living at Camara, an isolated location in the shadow of Lugnaquilla Mountain. When Dwyer was 12, the family circumstances improved somewhat; they moved to less remote Eadestown, near Baltinglass where they earned a living from sheep farming. As a Roman Catholic, Dwyer could not be educated formally and so attended a hedge school. These were small and originally illegal. They were aimed at providing a basic education to Catholic children. While the name hedge school suggests teaching took place in the open-air, classes were normally held indoors in cabins and barns with the standard of learning often surprisingly high. Certainly, Dwyer possessed sufficient education to become, in later life, a high-ranking public servant.

When Dwyer was 19 years old, the Society of United Irishmen was established in Belfast, mostly by well-to-do Protestants and dissenters with the aim of achieving parliamentary reform. When hopes of such reform faded, the Society became more militant and republican. As the movement spread nationwide, it was inspired by the relatively recent American War of Independence and the ongoing French Revolution. It was the first and only Irish revolutionary brotherhood to attract large numbers of followers from all religious groupings. Seeing an Irish Republic as a way to religious freedom, the Society was soon embraced by many adherents to the Roman Catholic faith.

Suppressed in 1794, the organisation re-invented itself as a secret oath-bound society aimed at achieving an independent Irish republic and soon after swept through the country like a forest fire.

Dwyer's hedge school teacher, Peter Burr, was a Trinity College educated Protestant who, nevertheless, held liberal and republican views. A strong influence on Dwyer, he was one of the first in the local area to set an example by joining the new organisation. Soon after, his pupil followed suit. It is unsurprising that in the climate of the time a young man from the disenfranchised Catholic majority, which had been completely subjugated for a century, would be drawn to the United Irishmen's radical programme of ending British rule and founding an independent, egalitarian republic.

Following in the footsteps of the American Colonists by throwing off the imperial yoke was clearly an inspirational vision that was now being eagerly embraced by the oppressed majority in Ireland. It was, however, always going to be easier to achieve for a large, resource-rich country almost 5000km away, which already possessed a trained and loyal local militia that could form the basis of a standing army that would fight British rule. By contrast, Ireland was a small, poverty-stricken nation close by Britain, where the local militias were almost entirely loyal to the crown. As one might expect from such circumstances, the Rising was to prove a big ask for the rebels.

In a rising climate of sectarian fear among the loyalist community, a campaign of terror was instigated against the new society. The local ignition point for rebellion came when 38 men were brutally executed in the West Wicklow village of Dunlavin including a close relative of Dwyer for their alleged United Irishman sympathies. This slaughter fanned the flames of hostility towards those seen as loyal to Britain. Historian, Ruan O'Donnell in his 1998 book *The Rebellion in Wicklow* states, "The Dunlavin executions, including that of John Dwyer of Seskin, affected Dwyer deeply and the killings instilled in him a thirst for revenge, which was left unsatisfied right up to the time of his ultimate surrender in December 1803."

Likely motivated by both idealism and a desire for revenge, Dwyer fought in the 1798 Rising with, according to contemporary accounts, remarkable bravery. He was a junior officer under General Joseph Holt in battles at Arklow, Vinegar Hill, Ballyellis and Hackettstown, with Ballyellis proving the only victory. After the defeat of the rebels and apparently fearing reprisals, Dwyer refused to accept a general amnesty for those who were not among the main leaders.

Instead, he withdrew with Holt and a band of rebels to the relative security of the Wicklow Mountains. From this redoubt amid Ireland's most extensive upland area, he continued to support the campaign of resistance to British rule in Ireland, while also taking time out to marry a local woman, Mary Doyle, in October 1798. After the failed French invasion of Connacht in September 1798, Holt saw the writing on the wall and surrendered to the British. Dwyer refused to do so, however, and continued to harass crown forces from the deep valleys in the south of Wicklow and thus earned himself the sobriquet "Outlaw of Glenmalure". Soon he became a highly romanticised figure and beacon of light for Irish Republicans when all else seemed lost after the debacle of the Rising.

According to his biographer, Chris Lawlor "Dwyer, who realised that pitched battles had been disastrous, was probably the first Irish rebel leader to employ 'hit and run tactics', with rebel leaders such as Michael Collins and Dan Breen citing Dwyer as an inspiration for their own guerrilla campaigns during the War of Independence a hundred and twenty years or so later." Certainly, his tactic of striking and then melting away would be a model for combat perfected by IRA man Tom Barry in his West Cork campaign.

Although none of his attacks on crown forces were militarily significant, Dwyer was a huge irritant to the administrators of British rule in Ireland. In a backhanded compliment to his effectiveness, one of the first purpose-built roads in Ireland was constructed through the Wicklow Mountains in order to subjugate him. Up to this point, the only roads in Wicklow ran east/west but now a new highway would lead north/south through the spine of the county. The route was modelled on the network of military roads, constructed by General Wade in Scotland, which were aimed at subjugating the rebellious Highlands. These well-built highways connected the military garrisons at Perth, Fort William, Fort Augustus and Fort George that were sent to Scotland following the unsuccessful Jacobite rebellion.

These days, it boggles the imagination to consider the number of hoops, in the form of objections and planning appeals, that would need to be negotiated in order to build the Wicklow Military Road through a pristine wilderness. Those were simpler times, however, and the new highway was constructed by a surveyor named Alexander Taylor without any recourse to such incidentals as planning permissions or the purchase of land. A canny Scot and apparent workaholic, Taylor maintained a thriving private practice while building the new road and also took on the task of surveying the post roads of Ireland. With the Military Road still to be completed, he took on the lucrative office of Chief Paving Commissioner for Dublin in 1807. He was outstandingly adept at expanding his income, but this ultimately led to his downfall. In 1817, a commission found discrepancies in monies he had approved for the postal survey. Then, in a sad echo of more recent happenings in Ireland, an inquiry found that Taylor had drawn off considerable sums of money from the Paving Board for his own personal use. He did not contest these allegations and was summarily removed from office. He died shortly afterwards while living in Naas, Co. Kildare.

Today, Taylor's Military Road is entirely used for peaceful purposes, mainly by tourists and hillwalkers wishing to access the Wicklow uplands. It traverses some of the most sublimely beautiful countryside in Ireland, so now let us set out to explore it. From our starting place in Rathfarnham, Co. Dublin, we head steeply into the Dublin Mountains and soon come to the carpark for the famous hunting lodge that has since become known as the Hellfire Club. Such a deliciously satanic appellation will prove too much of a temptation, so we will abandon the auto here and trundle up the forest paths to visit the famous club, which stands atop Montpelier Hill overlooking Dublin.

This edifice was built by William Conolly (known as Speaker Connolly), an extremely wealthy 18th Century politician who also constructed the famous Palladian mansion at Castletown, Co. Kildare. Apparently his first mistake was that the stone used in building, what was originally a hunting lodge, was pillaged from earlier burial tombs. The spirits resident in the tomb were apparently none too pleased about being disturbed and decided to haunt the new building. After Connolly's death, the hunting lodge is said to have become a meeting place for the Irish Hellfire Club. This was a secret organisation that was dedicated to all manner of debauchery including satanism whose members had apparently been barred from the taverns of Dublin.

You will probably agree with me here that the building has a somewhat eerie feel to it with its stone roof and gloomy interior. On a dark night it would certainly make an ideal place for dabbling in the occult, but on sunny days it is invariably busy with recreationists attracted by the expansive views across Dublin City. Nothing ever appears to run a smoothly in Ireland, and at the time of writing, a €19m plan for a visitor centre, café and additional walks was being opposed by local residents and conservationists who believe that the development would consist of over-tourism. We will have time to discuss the merits and demerits of this proposal as we return downhill to our parking place.

Onwards now over the shoulder of Kilakee Mountain before we descend through sublimely isolated moorlands into secluded

Glencree, where you will probably find it difficult to believe that such an unspoiled wilderness could exist just a few minutes' drive from the Dublin suburbs. Immediately, it will become obvious that a huge effort, and a not inconsiderable expense, was invested in subduing Dwyer, for the road does not serve any meaningful population area.

Reaching the valley, another austere looking building will grab the eye. This was the first in a series of barracks that were located along the Military Road, but abandoned soon after as the Wicklow countryside became more peaceful and the threat of a French invasion receded. It was then used for a time as a reformatory school for troubled teenagers run by a religious order known as the Oblates of Mary Immaculate. While the Catholic Church undoubtedly has much to answer for when it came to the custody of vulnerable children entrusted to its care, it is worth noting here the contribution it made to preserving Ireland's built heritage. Many large buildings, including some of the great houses of Ireland, were saved from inevitable destruction when taken over by the Church and run as schools on which no property taxes or death duties were payable.

Later used as a reception centre for German children being fostered in Ireland after the Second World War, the building rose again in the 1970s as the famous Glencree Centre for Peace and Reconciliation. This institution has done much good work to bring peace and understanding to many troubled places across the world and in particular to the two religious communities in Northern Ireland.

Traversing a totally unpopulated upland, our route climbs out of Glencree to become the highest public road in Ireland at 523m. The landscape here will likely prompt the thought of how totally inaccessible and ungovernable this area would have been prior to building the road. Next, we will come upon the two picturesque Lough Brays between which a track blossoms steeply upwards towards a rocky prow known as Eagles Crag. Having ascended on a number of occasions to this redoubt, I can assure you it offers sublime views east across the pristine vastness of the Wicklow Mountains National Park to the Irish Sea, and the distant mountains of Snowdonia shimmering beyond. Needing to push on, however, we will be obliged to leave this excursion for another day and continue south by a bridge over the nascent River Liffey to gain the Sally Gap.

Next comes the most isolated section of the Military Road which is the part that will convey us to Laragh village. The main reward along this section is scenic Glenmacnass waterfall – a spectacular 80-metre, triple-drop cascade situated at the head of the Glenmacnass Valley. You will notice here how the hardness of the granite has prevented the waters from eroding the rocky base and thus making the fall more vertical. This is what invariably happens with softer rocks, where waterfalls tend to continually move upstream through a process of erosion.

From Laragh, the route doglegs over a pass between Kirikee and Cuilentragh Mountain. Near the top of the pass, we will come upon the simple granite monument to the memory of international cyclist, Shay Elliott. At a time when internationally famous Irish sports stars are almost two-a-penny, you will, perhaps, have difficulty understanding that within the introverted world of 1960s Ireland such individuals were rare as hens' teeth, in what was an international backwater. Elliot was certainly one of the few who brought a sense of glamour and excitement to the dreary Ireland of his day and helped the Irish people build self-confidence as they prepared to join what is now the European Union. Although a latecomer to the sport of cycle racing, Elliott was one of the very few sportsmen from Ireland of this period to achieve international acclaim. Renowned for his speedy ascents of mountain roads, he enjoyed many famous victories across Europe and was the first English speaking person to win a stage of the Tour de France and also the first to wear the race leader's yellow jersey. His death in 1971 at the early age of 36, came about in unclear circumstances and resulted from a gunshot wound.

From the monument, we descend into the Dwyer stronghold at Glemalure where there is a large monument dedicated to the outlaw's memory and further up the valley a granite slab inscribed with names of those who fought alongside him. Then, it is over the final high pass on the eastern flanks of Lugnaquilla Mountain before the Military Road terminates near the tiny village of Aghavannagh. Here, another military barracks was built. After the soldiers departed, the building eventually came into the possession of Charles Stewart Parnell and later was the home of Irish Parliamentary Party leader, John Redmond.

You will now have seen that the new road was a considerable investment for its time – it actually cost about one thousand pounds per mile to construct. Although not fully completed during the time of Dwyer's rebellion, it meant that the writing was on the wall for the Outlaw of Glenmalure. Troops could now be stationed in new barracks built at Glencree, Glendalough, Glenmalure and Aughavannagh. This greatly diminished Dwyer's freedom of manoeuvre in his mountain fastness which meant that by the time the Military Road was completed in 1809 it was already obsolete for there were by then no rebels in Wicklow to subdue. This will probably have you wondering what was the future for the Wicklow Outlaw. The answer is a surprisingly lengthy one for the story of Michael Dwyer's later life contains as many twists as an Irish boreen and would probably be considered too unbelievable if proposed for a book of fiction.

Ultimate success in his campaign against British rule depended on a French intervention in Ireland. This beacon of hope was a hugely motivating factor for the rebels but became an increasingly unlikely prospect as time passed. The imbroglio of Robert Emmet's rising in 1803, which Dwyer wisely refused to support, turned out to be little more than a street riot. It achieved nothing but the execution of the leaders and an impassioned speech from the dock by an unrepentant Emmet exhorting following generations to continue the quest for Irish Independence. However, it resulted in the re-imposition of martial law, which greatly threatened the freedom of the Wicklow rebel by putting ever more pressure on his followers and kinsmen in the community. According to Chris Lawlor, Dwyer's guerrilla warfare was having a detrimental effect on the economy of Dunlavin parish and of west Wicklow generally while additionally he states "The military also pursued a campaign of arrests against known or suspected friends and relations of Dwyer, straining his kinship network almost to breaking point".

It was now becoming increasingly dangerous to give shelter to Dwyer and his diminishing band of followers, so the outlaw was forced to rely more on improvised shelters in the high mountains. With his support base and area of operation now hugely threatened and the local community being rapidly impoverished, Dwyer soon recognised the end game had arrived. He decided to seek terms for peace from the liberal-minded local MP, Lord William Hume of Humewood Castle, Kiltegan, Co. Wicklow. In return, Hume appears to have given assurances that Dwyer and his wife Mary would both be allowed free passage to America.

Hume failed - or was unable - to deliver on this promise and instead Dwyer was incarcerated in Kilmainham Gaol on a charge of treason. He was never formally tried. Instead, he was informed in August 1805 that he was being banished for life, to New South Wales in Australia. Not having been convicted of any crime he would, however, go as a free man. Later that month, he set sail from Queenstown, Co. Cork, never to set eyes on his native shores again. He was aboard a ship known as the *Tellichery* that was bound for Botany Bay and was accompanied on the voyage by his wife, older children and some close acquaintants from his rebel days.

Arriving to Australia in February 1806, the rebels were each awarded one hundred acres of land. Having escaped death by a whisker on many occasions, this is where Dwyer might have been expected to settle down for a life of peaceful prosperity. Unfortunately, a new governor of New South Wales was appointed as he arrived. Already well-known for a famous mutiny by the crew of the Bounty, when he was that ship's captain, William Bligh was a strict disciplinarian with, it appears, little time for Irish rebels. In May 1807, Dwyer found himself accused of plotting to seize the colony. It seems improbable that the Irishman would have, in a mere 15 months, found his feet to the extent of leading a rebellion in a strange land he barely knew. Perhaps, it was his previous record as an outlaw that stood against him and his arrest may have been a pre-emptive strike by Bligh. After what appeared to have been merely a show trial, Dwyer was convicted and shipped off to the tiny, remote and brutal penal colony on Norfolk Island. Six months later he was transferred to Tasmania.

This should have closed the book on Dwyer's remarkable life, but there was yet another extraordinary twist of fate. Bligh had a track record of getting under people's skin and conflict with the colonists culminated in yet another mutiny, known as the "Rum Rebellion". In 1808, Major George Johnston marched his soldiers on Government House in Sydney to arrest Bligh and install a new governor. With the departure of Bligh, Michael Dwyer was soon after pardoned and released from captivity to resume his life near Sydney

Like many transported Irish rebels who were to follow him, he soon became part of the establishment, and, in a classic example of poacher turned gamekeeper, the former 'Outlaw of Glenmalure' was, in 1810, appointed a police constable. Clearly, he was well regarded in the colony, for he was appointed Chief Constable for Liverpool, New South Wales, in 1920. Ironic as it may seem, Dwyer was now a servant of the Crown and an upholder of the law he had once so bitterly opposed; but there was to be no happy ending.

Dismissed from the Constabulary for drunken conduct and

maladministration, Dwyer was forced to sell off most of his assets. This included a tavern named The Harrow Inn, where he was reputed to have been his own best customer. Now bankrupt, he was incarcerated in a debtors' prison. Here he apparently contracted dysentery, to which he succumbed in August 1825, a short time after his release.

Originally interred at Liverpool, Dwyer's remains were reburied to mark the centenary of the 1798 rebellion in Waverley Cemetery, Sydney. It was estimated by a contemporary newspaper account in the Sydney Freeman's Journal that a crowd of 200,000 attended with the Cardinal-Archbishop of Sydney stating, "Michael Dwyer had not lost his life in the cause of his country, but he had bravely faced every peril, and gave abundant proof of heroic patriotism in his efforts to redress his country's wrongs."

And it isn't just in Australia that Dwyer continues to be held in high regard with many heroic tales recounted of his deeds. For 19th Century Irish Nationalists, there was no disguising the fact that the 1798 and 1803 rebellions had both been abysmal failures. The principal leaders were all executed or, in the case of Wolfe Tone, died in captivity. At a time when Irish nationalism was reviving itself, Dwyer offered the only true beacon of heroic resistance that the vastly superior forces of the crown had been unable to capture or subjugate.

It is, therefore, unsurprising that nationalist leaders propagated and indeed embellished the myth of "the Wicklow Chieftain" with his human frailties being ignored or transformed into positives. None more so then in a poem written in heroic style by Nationalist MP and onetime Lord Mayor of Dublin, T.D. Sullivan, which did much to build the myth of Dwyer. Here, the incident where he and his followers imposed themselves on local families at Derrynamuck with Dwyer then miraculously escaping an encirclement, mainly through good fortune and probable incompetence by the soldiers, is recounted as if it was inevitable due to Dwyer's almost superhuman attributes.

Today, we can take a more sanguine view of Dwyer the man. Undoubtedly, he was an individual who lived life on the edge and was clearly attracted to the road less travelled. In an extraordinary life, he rose from poverty to become, even within his own lifetime, a great Irish hero and later a remarkable success in Australia. Only a man gifted with many talents and a streak of ruthlessness could have overcome the adversities Dwyer faced in his lifetime.

The most extraordinary fact about Dwyer was his ability to evade capture for over five years in the Wicklow uplands despite, at one time, having a bounty on his head of 500 guineas (about €50,000 in today's values). It has, however, been said there are only ruthless revolutionaries and failed revolutionaries and without doubt Dwyer could – in common with later Irish rebels such as Michael Collins and Liam Lynch – be merciless when required. According to Chris Lawlor "Children, women, invalids – Dwyer either shot them or had them shot if he thought they posed a threat or would inform on him." We can, therefore, speculate that it was a combination of both genuine loyalty and real fear among the local population that ensured this bounty was never collected.

Apparently, a born leader, he was never one to take a rear seat but seemed intent, at all times, on pushing back the boundaries of the possible. He took a decision to continue with the 1798 rebellion, when almost all others accepted a risky amnesty. He was, however, pragmatic enough to seek terms when his position became hopeless and later accept the role of Chief Constable in the service of the Crown. A combination of fondness for alcohol and a desire to achieve too much was probably the reason for his final undoing in Australia.

It is sometimes said that history doesn't predict the future but does allow us to better understand the present. There can be little doubt that Dwyer's poignant story of rags to fame and relative riches before returning to rags deserves its place in history. In the circumstances of his time, his support for the egalitarian, non-denominational United Irishmen was well justified and still points to a lesson for Irish society. Endowed with a vastly resilient personality, his heroic stand in the Wicklow Mountains was motivated by idealism rather than personal gain. This idealism would go on to inspire many future generations of Irish rebels. His survival of the rebellion and eventful time in Australia provided an early heroic figure around whom the Irish diaspora would unify and identify.

To mark the bicentenary of the end of Dwyer's five-year guerrilla campaign in Wicklow a statue in his honour was unveiled by the Irish Taoiseach of the day, Bertie Ahern, in the Glen of Imaal on December 14, 2003. It was the first statue of Dwyer to be erected and is situated about half a mile from where he grew up. This statue should act as a reminder to future generations that the exploits of Michael Dwyer gave hope to Irish people during some of the, soon to follow, darkest decades of Ireland's history.

# CHAPTER 6

# The Mountain Monastery

I n 1830 a Waterford man arrived back in Ireland seeking sanctuary. He was from Ballybricken near Waterford City but for many years had been a Cistercian monk in Brittany. Ironically for such a nominally Catholic country, the Cistercian Order had just come through a torrid time in France as a consequence of the Revolution. Expelled from France by the new populist government, the monks spent time exiled to both Switzerland and Russia. Eventually, they managed to re-establish themselves at Melleray Abbey in Brittany, but they had only just about got their feet under the pews when another anti-clerical government followed upon the Second French revolution. It decreed that all English and Irish monks should be excluded from France.

Fr Vincent Ryan had been forced to leave Ireland to become a Cistercian monk since there were no monasteries in Ireland during the early part of the 19th Century. He had, however, long held a dream to restore the Cistercian Order to Ireland. Now the French Government had provided an urgent reason to do so. Ryan was dispatched to his native country with the mission to find a suitable place for the soon-to-be expelled monks. When he arrived back in Ireland, he found a land where freedom of religious practice had finally returned, but a countryside that was almost entirely in the hands of Protestant landowners. With a population of more than 8 million to feed, good quality land was in short supply.

Generous patrons happy to endow large tracks of land, which had been such a feature of past Cistercian life in Ireland, were now rather thin on the ground. Not being a mendicant order, farmland was urgently required as a source of income for the incoming Cistercians in order that they could survive. With typical monastic industry he checked out sites in Kildare and Galway that proved unsuitable. On the advice of a contact he made through the Irish Liberator, Daniel O'Connell, he even undertook the long journey to West Mayo to inspect what turned out to be an unsaleable blanket bog. In desperation he was forced to rent a small holding at Rathmore, Co. Kerry, and it was only just in time. Soon after, 64 monks who had been expelled from France arrived on board a French warship to Cobh, Co. Cork, where they were given an enthusiastic reception by the townspeople. They quickly discovered, however, the land holding and house at Rathmore were inadequate for the needs of such a large community, so the search for a permanent monastic site continued.

Then, Vincent Ryan heard reports of land that might be available at Scrahan in his native Co. Waterford. He travelled to investigate and was not impressed.

> There were 600 acres of land in the tract, it is true, but it was mountain land in the strictest sense of the term, rough and uneven in surface, covered with a thick dark growth of heather, furze and rushes; there were patches, too, where the heavy rains or the mighty force of mountain streams had washed away the thin surface of the peat and left nothing but the naked rock. Not a tree was to be seen over the whole extent of the area, nor a ditch nor a fence nor even a building of any kind except for a dilapidated gamekeeper's lodge.
>
> –*The History of Mount Melleray Abbey* by Stephen J. Moloney, p.9

The fact that this land had remained underused amid the huge population pressures in the lead up to the Great Famine spoke for itself. Nevertheless, the situation was desperate for the Cistercians and this might be the best land on offer in an impoverished country.

The difficulties experienced by monastic orders in the 19th Century contrast starkly with the medieval period. It was then that a relatively innocuous event occurred which would have a profound effect on European history. In 1113, a 22-year-old minor nobleman named Bernard of Fontaines, who hailed from Burgundy, entered a community of monks at a new monastery at Citeaux Abbey near Dijon in France. We can safely assume he didn't do this in pursuit of an easier life. The community he joined were originally Benedictines governed by the austere rule of their founder. Believing the observance of these rules had become lax in their own order at Molesme Abbey, they had founded Citeaux 15 years earlier with the goal of following more closely the rule of St Benedict - the founder of western monasticism.

Over time, they drifted away from the Benedictines, changed from black to white habits made from undyed sheep's wool and became known as the Cistercians or White Monks. Vegetarian before the word had even entered the lexicon, the life pursued by these monks was one of the most extreme frugality. Prominent in the rule of the new abbey was the return to manual work, especially long hours spent labouring in the fields, which has become a defining feature of Cistercian life ever since. A life centred entirely on God that was lived in an atmosphere of silence was never going to be an easy calling. Bernard was, however, immediately enthralled by the simplicity and frugality of monastic living.

In 1115, he was sent with a group of other monks to found a new monastery at Clairvaux in Eastern France. Here, he became the highly charismatic abbot of an enclosed order with the strictest observance of the rule of St Benedict. You might expect the unrelenting life of work, self-denial and rising at 2am to pray would have made the recruitment of monks something of a headache for the young abbot. But not at all; Bernard had now morphed into a religious superstar. The new austerity he preached had captured the zeitgeist and his main headache involved the large numbers flocking to join the Clairvaux community. Never a man to let grass grow under his feet, Bernard quickly found a solution, which has been copied by many Cistercian Abbots ever since. He eased the overcrowding at Clairvaux by dispatching groups of the new Cistercians to establish a network of daughter houses across Europe.

In 1140, St Malachy, the Irish Archbishop of Armagh, was experiencing his own headache with the urgent need to reform the Celtic Church and bring it under the authority of Rome. On his way to Rome, he visited the now famous Clairvaux Abbey in search of a solution and immediately hit it off with Bernard. The two became close friends, so close in fact that they would eventually be buried in the same grave. Impressed with the discipline and work ethic of the Cistercians and no friend of the indigenous Celtic monasteries who largely followed their own rules, Malachy came to believe that introducing European monks to Ireland would help to dispel rampant corruption within Irish monasticism. He left four of his companions to be trained in monastic discipline at Clairvaux. On his return to Ireland, he founded Mellifont, the first Irish Cistercian Abbey, which was soon sprouting a series of daughter houses.

The Norman invasion accelerated the process of Irish monastery building. The invaders had the support of the Pope who, unimpressed with the intransigence of the Irish Church, gave the King of England dominion over the "barbarous nation" of Ireland. The Pontiff saw this as a useful way of bringing into line the Irish Church, who were committing the monumental sin of paying nothing to Rome. So, the incoming Cistercians became the dedicated foot-soldiers of the movement to Romanise Irish Christianity. The Celtic monasteries quickly perished on the vine as the new order spread across Ireland with the rapidity of a forest fire.

It soon became apparent the Cistercians literally knew their onions. They showed a strong preference for the fertile, crop friendly soils east of the River Shannon, which they rendered vastly productive. Obtaining such land presented few difficulties, however, Irish kings, chiefs and Norman lords queued up with endowments of their best property for the prestige of having a monastic establishment. Cistercianism had truly captured the spirit of the age.

Now the similarity between the early Cistercians and Irish airline Ryanair may not immediately seem blindingly obvious. The secret of Cistercian success came, however, in the way they "Ryanairised" their monasteries, at a time when the term "mechanistic system" had yet to be invented by organisation theorists. Just as every Ryanair airplane is today similar to all others, the Cistercians simplified things by building each monastery to a common plan; a cruciform church on the north side of the abbey was built adjacent to a cloister for private prayer. The chapter house and rooms where the monks lived and ate were grouped around the cloister with other more functional buildings detached from the main abbey. Similar to the Ryanair business model, the new monasteries were utilitarian and largely without ornamentation, but controlled by a centralised structure. It was no-frills worship before the term had been invented and - like Ryanair - the model proved unstoppable in its march across Europe.

Soon there were more than 40 Cistercian monasteries across Ireland that were almost identical to each. Unlike the orders who arrived later to Ireland such as the Franciscans and Augustinians, the Cistercian abbeys were built far from towns and as a rule, the monks did not involve themselves in pastoral ministry. Each Cistercian monastery was a complete world in itself, and this consequent requirement for self-sufficiency created an urgent need for innovation in order to survive. To the local people in a sparsely populated countryside with few large buildings, the new monasteries must have seemed like enormous, awe-inspiring edifices that spoke of spiritual power. They were certainly great centres of industry, innovation and local employment. Villages that housed workers and craftsmen sprang up alongside the abbeys, serving as a reminder that, during the medieval period, most technological advances in Europe emerged from the monasteries.

One of the new Irish Cistercian monasteries became a renowned centre for medieval pilgrimage. The sliver of the Holy Rood (true cross) was reputedly brought to Ireland by Queen Isabella of Angoulême, who was the widow of England's King John. She is said to have bestowed it on a Cistercian Monastery near Thurles, Co. Tipperary. This Abbey then became known as Holycross and with the passage of time transformed into a great destination for pilgrimage - a tradition that survived beyond the Reformation and well into the 17th Century.

Pilgrimage was undoubtedly the great ecclesiastical cash cow of the medieval period and, as evidence of the strong pilgrim tradition to Holycross, the well-known archaeologist Peter Harbison has suggested that the extensive building works that took place at the Abbey during the 15th Century were funded by pilgrim donations. This suggestion seems very plausible, for whenever I visit Holycross what strikes me is how ornate it is by comparison with the generally minimalist Cistercian standard of decoration. Immediately obvious are the beautifully intricate examples of artwork in stone, which certainly wouldn't have come cheap. Outstanding examples are at the shrine, which is believed to have held the true cross in Medieval times and on the wonderful sedilia beside the high altar.

In the end, the Cistercians became victims of their own industry and success. Many of the abbeys were extremely wealthy, particularly from the wool trade, since everybody in those days wore woolen garments. Each abbey possessed a large tract of land, and at its peak the Cistercians are estimated to have owned about half-a-million acres in Ireland, with the consequent problem of political interference in the appointment of abbots.

In the 16th Century, this wealth did not go unnoticed by such a famously lavish spender as King Henry VIII. His break with Rome and the abuses that had crept into many of the monasteries gave Henry the perfect opportunity to raise some badly needed cash. Although remaining a lifelong adherent to the Catholic, but not the Roman Catholic, faith he now declared himself head of the church in England. Then, dissolving the monasteries across his entire kingdom, he used their wealth to pay for his expansive lifestyle and many wars.

Despite grandiosely having himself crowned King of Ireland, Henry did not directly control the north and west of the country and so the dissolution of the Irish monasteries took longer. Occupying great swathes of fertile land in the east and south, the Cistercians were first in his line of fire, but the other monastic orders soon followed. By the middle of the 16th Century the Tudor reconquest and the coming of Oliver Cromwell, who vehemently disliked Catholicism, ensured that monastic communities had entirely disappeared from the Irish landscape.

The Cistercians would be impossible to forget, however, for they had endowed Ireland with a rich, if minimalist, architectural heritage. As the first European order to reach Ireland, they left an indelible mark, particularly in Leinster and East Munster, with austere but beautifully formed abbeys such as those at Dunbrody, Holycross, Jerpoint and Tintern, but it would be a two-century wait for the tenuous re-establishment of the order with the return to Ireland of Vincent Ryan.

The guesthouse at Mount Melleray Abbey, Co. Waterford is, as always, a haven of calm and solitude in a frenetic world. A long tradition holds that it is still possible to come and stay in any Cistercian Abbey in return for an unspecified donation. With me is the abbey librarian, Fr Uinseann O'Maidin. Modest and resolutely in the moment, he immediately displays an expansive grasp of Cistercian history. A Limerick City man, he joined the Cistercian Order at the age of 17, and apart from five years spent with the Cistercians in Rome, has been at Melleray ever since. My first question is, how did he come to join the Cistercians? "My father used to come here to stay from time to time when I was young. I came with him when I was about 14 and liked what I saw. After that, the idea of joining the Cistercians was always in the back of my mind. Then, when I was 17 God called me, it's as simple as that."

But how did the Abbey itself come to exist at this unlikely location on the slopes of the Knockmealdown Mountains? "It's a long story", says Fr Uinseann. "After a short time in Rathmore, Vincent Ryan was told by Fr Patrick Fogarty about a tract of mountain land that was on offer to the Cistercians at Srahan, Cappoquin, Co. Waterford. The land was owned by Sir Richard Keane who believed the coming of the Cistercians would also attract other businesses to an impoverished area. Vincent Ryan went to see it and since the land was the best on offer, a price was agreed."

This triggers the thought that building a monastery in pre-famine Ireland must have been a mammoth task for penniless monks, so I asked Father Uinseann how was it achieved. "The local communities flocked to the monks' aid. Thousands of men from the surrounding parishes came to donate a day's labour to the new foundation. Work went ahead quickly and 1838 saw the dedication of the new monastic church, which was the first in Ireland since the Reformation," explained Fr Uinseann. "Soon after, Vincent Ryan, our founder, was elected Dom Vincent when he became Abbot of what had now become Mount Melleray Abbey - the first person to hold such a title in Ireland for more than two centuries."

It was Shakespeare who said that, "When sorrows come, they come not single spies, but in battalions". I can't help thinking how true this was for the Mount Melleray Cistercians. Having been excluded from France, the new order was scarcely settled in Ireland when the Great Famine struck; the potato crop, on which ordinary people depended, failed disastrously. So, I questioned Fr Uinseann about the inevitable difficulties that must have been caused by the Famine. "You must remember that at that time Mount Melleray was still a very poor establishment, but the monks did what they could to feed the local people", said Fr Uinseann. "Dom Vincent gave instructions that no person in need should be sent away unaided as long as there was a morsel of food in the house. There was a bin at the gates from which meal was distributed to nearly 100 people each day and local tradition holds that miraculously this bin, which is still in the possession of the Abbey, never emptied."

The third Abbot of Mount Melleray was Bruno Fitzpatrick, who would also make a huge impression. Born in Co. Westmeath, he entered the Cistercian Order in May 1843, having previously taken holy orders as a secular priest, and then rose rapidly to become Abbot of Mount Melleray in 1848. The order was lucky because he proved the ideal man for the job. He presided over the consolidation and expansion of the Abbey; he also founded a junior seminary for prospective priests. A new Melleray was established in Iowa, U.S.A., and in 1878, Mount Saint Joseph's Abbey in Co. Offaly – the Cistercians were truly back in Ireland.

A golden era for the Cistercians was to follow that would last for about a century. In this period, two more daughter houses of Mount Melleray were established at Mellifont Abbey, Co. Louth and Portglenone, Co. Antrim. In the light of this, I asked Fr Uinseann what it was like when he first joined Mount Melleray in the new heyday of Irish Cistercianism.

"I first joined the Order on August 15, 1949, the Feast of the Assumption, never having been away from home for any length of time previously. I remember it was a very busy place then – there were about 135 monks and the students from the junior seminary were all around us, but there was also a great sense of prayerful solitude with an atmosphere of silence that I immediately liked. In those days we only spoke for totally necessary reasons. I would have spent long periods without uttering a word so there was plenty of time for personal prayer and contemplation. This was before the Second Vatican Council and so the rules were quite strict. Sometimes, I found it difficult, but remember I had no basis of comparison with any other life. This helped. After the Second Vatican Council, things got easier: we were now able to do things because we wanted to and not because we had to." As an example, he tells me that he now has a mobile phone but, intriguingly, has never actually used it.

But when he transferred to Rome in the early 1980s, the Eternal City must surely have seemed a huge contrast with the solitude of monastic life amid the Knockmealdown Mountains. "It was indeed, and the first year amid all the hustle and bustle was quite difficult. However, the work as a secretary to the Order was interesting and gradually I settled in, but I always wanted to return to Mount Melleray."

With the junior seminary long closed at the Abbey due to the fall in vocations and only eight monks now remaining, I ask Fr Uinseann about the future for Mount Melleray? "Worldwide in every order, there is a crisis of vocations and the Cistercians are no exception. I can't see into the future but I don't believe Mount Melleray will close. I take great comfort from the fact that God has said he will be with us until the end of time. He will provide for us as he always has. I don't worry about it; I will simply accept whatever is God's will."

Afterwards I ramble around the impeccably maintained grounds of the Abbey to get a feel for the place. The buildings are indeed sublimely captivating, but ludicrously huge and high maintenance for housing just eight monks. Undoubtedly there is still the almost tangible sense of beauty and peace which has attracted the faithful - and indeed not so faithful - to Mount Melleray for almost two centuries.

Written bold, in large lettering, in the Church foyer is the exhortation from St Benedict "prefer absolutely nothing to the love of Christ". This I, rather cynically, conclude could be taken in two ways, which probably means I would have made a very unworthy Cistercian. Inside the beautifully evocative community church - with its magnificent stained-glass window behind the high altar - my cynicism quickly evaporates. There is a strong odour of incense hanging in the air and an undeniable feeling of sanctity and otherworldliness. Cistercians pray together seven times a day, and so I wait around to watch the eight monks and one novice file in for vespers (evening prayer).

The chanting is simple but hauntingly evocative, yet I feel a sense of sadness, for it is hard to know, despite Fr Uinseann's optimism, what will now become of Mount Melleray. A possibility exists that, for the second time in five centuries, the Cistercians will disappear from Ireland. You can't have an abbey without monks and the stream of new entrants has simply dried up. In a vastly more materialistic world, it seems there are no longer men who are prepared to live the life of hard work self-denial and communal prayer that Fr Uinseann has practiced for the past 70 years.

If the end of Cistercianism in Ireland is indeed imminent there will doubtless be many who will not mourn the end of the Order, regarding it as an anachronistic way of living that is now well past its sell-by date. I can't agree, however, for as I ramble in the calming solitude of the Abbey grounds, it seems these simple monks have a valuable lesson to teach us. They point resolutely to the fact that another way of life is possible that is neither materialistic nor self-serving. They force us to question the values we take for granted: the primacy of the individual, the unending quest for self-gratification and the frenzy towards conspicuous consumption. Perhaps we sometimes shut out what they have to say because they make us uncomfortable: they oblige us to face our own deep-seated doubts and insecurities about the true meaning of our lives.

Like most people, I know that I could never measure up to the exacting standards of obedience, poverty, work and prayer in an atmosphere of silence that is required from Cistercian monks. But even for those of us who are not particularly devout, religious life provides a valuable touchstone against which we can measure ourselves and stay grounded in reality. After speaking with Fr Uinseann, it seemed to me that the core belief of the monks at Mount Melleray is simply that true fulfilment comes not from the pursuit of wealth and happiness, but with a spiritual mindfulness and the act of serving. For this reason, and also because of the huge solace they have provided for troubled souls before the word counselling was invented, I hope that somehow Uinseann is right. It would indeed be good for believers and non-believers alike if the Cistercians were to remain a comforting presence at Mount Melleray Abbey as part, perhaps, of a new 21st Century iteration of monastic living.

# CHAPTER 7

# Tipperary's Fabled Mountain

There is something sublimely evocative about this mountain and today is no exception. In contrast to its bulkier and more angular neighbours - the Comeraghs and Galtees - it is an isolated eminence with a domed head and graceful flowing shoulders that was always destined to gather legends. Overlooking the surrounding Tipperary countryside like a benevolent grandmother, Slievenamon remains an ever-present backdrop for South Tipp folk as they go about their daily business.

As I ramble up the track, the mountainside is busy with recreationists of all kinds. These vary from power-walkers wafting easily upwards to those ascending as if their laces were tightly fastened together. On gaining open mountainside, almost everyone stops briefly to imbibe of the sublime vista immediately over the Suir Valley to the south before continuing upwards.

About halfway into the ascent, it is my custom to turn and gaze upon the forlorn skeletal remains of Kilcash Castle, which adorn the south-western slopes of the mountain. A famous poem titled "Caoine Cill Chais", which was once known to virtually every school child in Ireland, mourns the loss of the great forests around Kilcash Castle and the "good lady" who once lived there, with the first verse going thus:

> Cad a dhéanfaimid feasta gan adhmad?
> Tá deireadh na gcoillte ar lár;

níl trácht ar Chill Chais ná ar a teaghlach
is ní chluinfear a cling go bráth

Now what will we do without timber?
The last of the woods are down
There's no talk of Cill Chais or its family
And its bell will be struck no more

We tend to seek simple narratives from history, and I always assumed this was a 17th Century lament for the fall of Gaelic Ireland after the Battle of Kinsale. Surely, it had been written by one of the many itinerant Irish bards, who entertained in the great houses of the Irish clans and now lamented the passing of their meal ticket. Then, while pottering around Kilcash Castle, at a time when it was still open to the public, I met a local man who informed me the poem is much later and probably comes from the 19th Century. Not referring to a Gaelic family at all, he informed me, it was concerned instead with a branch of the great Anglo-Norman Butler family. Sure enough, when I checked it out, I found that, alas, he was on the button.

With their castles liberally strewn across the rich farmlands of Kilkenny and Tipperary, the Butlers were, for five centuries, by far the most powerful family in the south midlands. Descended from Theobald Fitzwalter, an English nobleman, the family came to Ireland in the 12th Century and were granted extensive lands in east Munster and south Leinster along with the title, Chief Butler of Ireland. Initially based at Gowran, Kilkenny Castle was purchased by James Butler, the 3rd Earl of Ormond, and became the family seat in 1381. The family was now comfortably situated in the middle of arguably Ireland's most fertile and productive county with their wealth initially based on the right to acquire 15% of the value of all wine imports into Ireland. With the royalist Butlers in charge,

Kilkenny was ranking close behind Dublin as the foremost seat of English power in Ireland.

One fascinating connection to the English monarchy is through Lady Margaret Butler who was born at Kilkenny, in the mid-15th Century. She married the wealthy Sir William Boleyn from Norfolk. The couple had ten children and their eldest son was Thomas Boleyn, father of Anne Boleyn, who became the ill-fated second wife of Henry VIII and short-lived Queen of England. She was, however, the mother of Queen Elizabeth I, who was, therefore, a great-grand-daughter of the Butlers and generally well disposed towards her Irish cousins.

Ostensibly the Butlers' job was to provide ample food and drink for the English King when he visited Ireland, but their real role was to remain loyal and serve English interests in Ireland. This, of course, was always going to be a rocky road to tread, but mostly the Butlers acquitted themselves admirably. Politically astute, the Butlers saw it in their interests to cooperate with the English monarchy rather than resist and thus managed to reap rich reward as royal favourites, while others among the great Anglo-Norman families floundered. Excellent at recognising which way the political winds were blowing, the Butlers entertained King James II, the last Catholic King of England, at their castle during the Jacobite wars in Ireland. After his defeat at the Battle of the Boyne, however, they were within a couple of weeks of welcoming the victor, James' protestant son-in-law, William of Orange, to Kilkenny.

Almost inevitably Kilcash Castle came into the possession of the ubiquitous Butlers in the 16th Century and became the redoubt of a Catholic branch of the clan. It remained in the ownership of the family until sold to the Irish State in 1997. The person eulogised in the poem "Caoine Cill Chais" as "the good lady most honoured and joyous of women" isn't some Gaelic noblewoman of generous disposition. Instead, it is the Countess Iveagh, who hailed from another great Anglo-Norman family of the 18th Century: The Burkes of

Clanricarde. Her second marriage was to Colonel Thomas Butler of Kilcash with whom she had eight children. She acquired her fame as a notable benefactor to Catholic clergy, the dispossessed and the travelling poets and bards at a time when the Penal Laws were at their most robust. She died at Kilcash in 1744.

The fall of Kilcash Castle had, however, nothing to do with her demise or indeed the decline in the 17th Century of Gaelic Ireland. It arose from much more mundane circumstances when the Protestant Dukes of Ormond in Kilkenny Castle had no heir to the title. John Butler (son of Countess Iveagh and a Catholic) then became the 17th Earl of Ormonde, when he inherited the Ormonde Earldom. He immediately moved to the family seat at Kilkenny Castle which, although badly in need of repair, still offered much more comfortable and centrally located surroundings. The family fortunes were quickly restored, however, when he astutely changed to the Protestant faith. This allowed him marry the wealthy heiress to the Castlecomer Coalfields, Anne Wandsworth, who then provided the finance for extensive restoration work on the castle. Surplus to requirements, the great Kilcash woods and landholdings were soon after sold and the once-proud stronghold was allowed fall into ruin.

However, the Butler dynasty continued. Unlike many of the other Irish clans, they had, through the turbulent Tudor period and later during the sectarian wars of the 16th Century, managed to keep their heads in every sense. When the right to levy a 15% tax on wine imports was finally revoked in 1811 the Crown paid a whopping £216,000 to buy it back. With this windfall, the family refurbished Kilkenny Castle to the grandeur we see today and thereby created a great tourism honeypot for Ireland's medieval city. With the coming of Irish independence, the Butler fortunes declined precipitously in the early 20th Century but they remained in possession of Kilkenny Castle up to the time it was acquired by Irish state for the princely sum of £50 in 1967.

The stony track up Slievenamon now trundles over a low rise and then to the summit. The going is never difficult, but is invariably demanding on the lungs. Surprisingly for such a salient peak, there is no cross adorning the top (721m) but, as compensation, there is a huge burial cairn, reputed to contain the entrance to the Celtic underworld.

A depression in the rocks is known locally as Fionn MacCumhaill's seat. Here, a wonderfully durable myth suggests that it was from this perch the legendary Irish mythical hero and leader of the Fianna warriors watched an abundance of hopeful candidates for his hand in marriage race to the summit. Legend has it he cheated and helped his favourite Gráinne, who was the daughter of Irish High King, Cormac mac Airt, to prevail. Having imbibed of the Salmon of Knowledge in his youth, Fionn was reputed to have thus acquired all the wisdom in the world. Not it seems when it came to the fairer sex. Certainly, he was not wise enough to give Gráinne a wide berth having failed to foresee that she would, unimpressed by his devotion, elope from the wedding banquet. Her paramour was the much younger Fianna warrior Diarmuid, who is reputed to have carried a love spot on his forehead that made him irresistibility attractive. The couple were then chased across Ireland by Fionn, which provided the material for the tragic stage and film melodramas of Diarmuid and Gráinne.

It was also on this spot that Waterford man Thomas Francis Meagher and Tipperary born Michael Doheny of the fledgling Young Ireland movement came in July 1848 to preach the doctrine of rebellion. They used the great symbolism of Slievenamon's summit to give a rousing speech to an estimated 50,000 people. Their stated purpose contained an implied threat to British rule in Ireland. According to the advance publicity, the objective of the meeting was to demonstrate "determination to obtain Irish independence by constitutional means if possible".

Earlier that year, Meagher had journeyed to France to study the revolution which was taking place there and returned with a flag of Ireland consisting of a green, white and orange tricolour. This was flown for the first time in Waterford on the 7 March 1848 with local tradition holding that it was also unfurled for the Slievenamon gathering. One fact is certain, however; it reappeared again during the 1916 Rising and then went on to be adopted as the national flag of the Irish Republic.

The immediate response by the authorities to the seditious Slievenamon gathering was the imposition of martial law. Then followed Ireland's contribution to the 1848 Year of Revolutions in Europe, which has since been dubbed the Battle of Widow McCormack's Cabbage Patch. Following a standoff with police at a widow's house near Ballingarry, Co. Tipperary, which was referred to by later revolutionaries as the 1848 Young Ireland Rebellion, the rebels soon fled. Doheny made his escape to New York while Meagher was arrested and exiled to Tasmania. He absconded and thereafter managed to reach New York.

Here, the highly erudite Meagher qualified as a lawyer. Rising to the rank of Brigadier-General in the US Army during the American Civil War, he afterwards became acting governor of the Montana Territory. Here, he developed the first constitution for the new State, before drowning by falling overboard from a steamboat on the Missouri River in what some considered suspicious circumstances.

The man who is, however, most associated with Slievenamon is Charles Kickham, whose family lived in the village of Mullinahone, which lies in the mountain's northern shadow. To most Tipperary people, Slievenamon is truly Kickham's mountain and when I was growing up in Co. Tipperary, there was a copy of his novel, *Knocknagow*, in virtually every sideboard. It was, in many ways, like Tolstoy's *War and Peace*: just about everybody wanted to have read it but not many wanted to actually read it. I remember having a valiant go at tackling it, since this was regarded as a sort of patriotic duty at the time. After a promising start, I found it complex and overlong, a bit like the curate's egg: good only in spots. With a multitude of plot twists and scenes that didn't seem to lead anywhere, it is probably a work that would have benefited from a good editor. I don't think I ever finished it.

Yet *Knocknagow* has colonised my imaginings ever since, when other more organised and competently written works have long been forgotten. The reason, I think, is the vivid descriptions of rural life and particularly the character of Mat the Thresher – a humble but noble and talented farm labourer. He defeats a representative of the local gentry in a sporting contest "for the credit of the little village" and so became a model for how rural people viewed their heroes in pre-EU Ireland.

The family, bearing the unusual sounding surname, originally came to Ireland as part of the Cromwellian conquest, but later changed their religion. By the early 19th Century the Kickhams were part of a relatively comfortable and growing Catholic middle class in Ireland. Charles Kickham was born in 1827 on the cusp of subtle but deep social change in Ireland. The Education Act of 1831 would soon make primary education universally available and greatly increase literacy in English at the expense of the Irish language. With the increased literacy, mass-circulation newspapers were beginning to make their appearance and would soon become the prime vehicle for politicising the populace, while railways would build awareness among ordinary people of the extended nation beyond their immediate community. Finally, the practice of Catholicism was moving from informal to highly formal. The newly resurgent Irish Church was imposing a new discipline on society and the practice of religion. Having witnessed the suppression of the Catholic Church that followed upon the French Revolution, it would soon become loud in its condemnation of the revolutionary societies with which Kickham would soon become deeply involved. Irish life was now being transformed by the resurgent Church into an extended exam. It could either be passed: go to heaven, or failed: go to hell. Members of revolutionary organisations were now placed firmly in the latter category and it took considerable fortitude for individuals to go against the dictates of the newly powerful Irish Church.

One individual who possessed this fortitude in spades was Charles Kickham. Growing to manhood at a time when the power and influence of Ireland's Liberator, Daniel O'Connell, was in sharp decline it is perhaps unsurprising that he soon came under the influence of the more radical Young Ireland movement. This group had split from O'Connell following his failure to win home rule for Ireland. Disillusioned at an early age by the perceived futility of parliamentary politics as demonstrated by the failure of O'Connell, Kickham was strongly attracted to the romantic nationalism as espoused by the poet Thomas Davis. As a young man he was peripherally involved with the abortive 1848 rebellion in Co. Tipperary, but managed to escape arrest by spending some time in hiding. Later, he became a founder member of the Irish Republican Brotherhood (IRB), which was dedicated to the establishment of an independent democratic republic in Ireland, by force of arms if necessary.

On the 15th of August 1863, Kickham, who suffered multiple health problems following upon an accident with gunpowder in his youth, climbed laboriously to Slievenamon's summit and there addressed a waiting crowd of about a thousand supporters. The event was probably worth the ascent by his audience for he told them what they wanted to hear by declaring that words alone would be useless in the struggle for freedom. Such views didn't go unnoticed, however. In 1865, Kickham was arrested and sentenced to 14 years imprisonment on a charge of treason-felony along with many of the other Fenian leaders. Released in 1869, because of poor health, he was soon back to his old ways as national chairman of the IRB executive.

Kickham was in many ways an enigmatic figure. A devout Roman Catholic he continually clashed with the Catholic Church during his lifetime, particularly with regard to its interventions in non-spiritual affairs. In common with most Irish revolutionary leaders, he possessed a tigerish wish to bring about an independent Ireland by force of arms, but displayed little interest in changing the underlying inequalities and power imbalances of society. A social conservative, he opposed the Land League - which had been founded by fellow Fenian Michael Davitt with the objective of enabling tenant farmers to own their land. Despite their many differences, he made common cause with the Catholic Church in condemning agrarian outrages and generally defended the right to private property. To this end, he regarded the Land League's 'No Rent Manifesto' against landlords as a communist conspiracy brought to the Irish countryside.

Kickham remained unmarried and died, while residing in Blackrock, Co. Dublin on 22 August, 1882. As a Fenian and vocal critic of the Catholic Church, his remains were not allowed into Thurles Cathedral when they arrived by train from Dublin and were reposed instead in the premises of Thomas Kirwin on Liberty Square. On the following day, no priest was in attendance for his burial in Mullinahone Cemetery.

Despite such clerical opposition and never having fired a shot in Ireland's cause, the generally mild-mannered Kickham is the man who, more than any other, has captured the spirit of Tipperary. In the years after his death he was considered by many the perfect model for the new nationalist Ireland. But it isn't for this he is most remembered today: instead, it is as a songwriter or balladeer.

The powerfully moving "Patrick Sheehan" is a vehemently anti-British ballad based on a real-life person. Sheehan was an ex-British soldier blinded in the Crimean war and then arrested for begging on Grafton Street. Sheehan wasn't, however, born in the sweetly pastoral Glen of Aherlow, as the ballad suggests, but in the more prosaic sounding Ennistymon, Co. Clare. "The Irish Peasant Girl" (She Lived Beside the Anner, at the Foot of Slievenamon) is also based on fact. The girl in question was Catherine Carew, a cousin and friend of Kickham from nearby Killusty. She emigrated to America at 17 and soon after died of consumption, but not before posting a poignant braid of her hair home to her mother in Ireland. His ballad of "Home Longings" has, however, become by far the most popular, and is now almost universally referred to by its alternative title "Slievenamon". It has been adopted as an unofficial anthem of Co. Tipperary and is almost guaranteed a rendition wherever Premier County folk gather at any place around the globe.

I now strike out west across the heathery mountainside. The going is a bit tedious but at least the underfoot conditions are dry so I have time for reflection. The thought occurs to me that, had we been contempories, I would probably have been one of the many to have admired Kickham for his courage, outspokenness, deep understanding of rural Ireland and refusal to become self-pitying in personal adversity. It is certainly easy to understand how he might have become radicalised, like so many others, upon witnessing the devastation unleashed by the Great Famine and the largely uncaring attitude of the British Government to what was then seen as merely an Irish problem.

Today, his books may appear to present an over sentimentalised view of rural Ireland, yet they are, like most great works of the imagination, steeped in the atmosphere of their time. It is important to remember that a rose-tinted view of Irish peasant life is exactly what his readers were demanding at the time and, to this end, he captured accurately the vivid idiom and singular mannerisms of 19th Century peasants. In the end, I conclude that he was a man ahead of his time: a republican living about a half-century before this idea became fashionable. Perhaps, he is best summarised with the oft-quoted description of Irish rebels: "the most conservative revolutionaries in history."

Descending quite rapidly until the moorland terrain levels out, I soon after go upwards again to gain a broad plateau. Here, it becomes apparent the mountain didn't totally escape cross-builders for about 2.5km from the summit, I reach Killusty Cross. This 8m high cross was erected to commemorate the 1950 Holy Year when the influence of Irish Catholicism was at its peak and there was a rash of hilltop cross building.

Standing beside this 60-year-old edifice, I enjoy extensive views over the Suir Valley and Clonmel. Beyond, the peaks of the Knockmealdown and Galtee Mountains stand shoulder-to-shoulder and remind me of a great rugby front row in scrum formation. This is the great horse-breeding country of South Tipperary and directly below me are the stout ramparts and attached horse breeding establishment of Kiltinan Castle. Dating from the 13th Century, it is one of the oldest continuously inhabited abodes in Ireland. Almost inevitably, it soon came into the hands of the Butler family, this time a branch known as the Dunboynes. As arch royalists, the Butlers of Kiltinan unsuccessfully led the resistance to the advance of the New Model Army in Ireland. Oliver Cromwell was not amused by this: the Dunboynes were summarily defenestrated from their estates, when Kiltinan was bombarded in 1650 with considerable damage caused to the structure. After being rebuilt as a manor house in the 18th Century by the Cooke family, it is, at the time of writing, owned by international composer and impresario Andrew Lloyd Weber, where he now runs a successful stud farm.

Moving west on a track that now descends, I reach a forest edge and continue left on an undulating, stony track that eventually crosses a small ravine before continuing to the enclosed lane leading to my parking place. As I drive away a thought strikes me about the decision not to execute the leaders of the Young Ireland Rebellion and the later Fenian Rising. As a result, these revolts quickly slipped from public consciousness with constitutional politics continuing to prevail well into the 20th Century. I couldn't help wondering, however, what would have been the outcome had a similarly humanitarian policy been pursued following the 1916 Rising. Nobody can ever supply a definitive answer to such tantalizing what-ifs, but this is what makes the study of history at once both fascinating and frustrating.

# CHAPTER 8

# The Desperate Escape to Gougane Barra

The time is near midnight and the men from the IRA's West Cork Flying Column are gazing into a darkened void. It is June 1920, and they are being hotly pursued by thousands of British soldiers who are sweeping in a great arc south and west through the Cork countryside, while other troops block the escape routes to Kerry. Standing atop the treacherous cliffs high in the Shehy Mountains over Gougane Barra, each volunteer is only too well aware that survival depends on finding a route to the pitch-black valley below.

Clearly, the odds are stacked against the IRA men, but morale remains high. Their commander is, after all, the charismatic Tom Barry who, in just eight months, had established an international reputation as an able, cunning and fearless guerrilla fighter. A hero in West Cork, he enjoys one considerable advantage: the unquestioning loyalty of the local population. Fearsome British reprisals against the citizens of West Cork have served to turn an initially wavering population firmly behind the Republican cause.

Against the vast resources of the British Empire, Barry's Flying Column consisted of only about 100 ill-trained volunteers and suffered from chronic shortages of arms, ammunition and equipment. However, Barry - unlike many of his predecessors in the struggle for Irish Independence - was no militarily naive revolutionary. Instead, he was an effective and ruthless fighter, committed to obliterating the enemy at all costs. To this end he had few scruples about peremptorily executing those - such as 16 alleged collaborators with British forces - whom he believed stood in the way of Irish freedom.

Born in 1897 at Langfors, Killorglin, Co. Kerry, the second of 14 children, Thomas Bernard Barry entered a family comfortable enough to employ a live-in servant. The son of an RIC constable he later moved with his family to Roscarbery in West Cork, when his father resigned from the police force. After running away from the prestigious Jesuit College at Mungret in Co. Limerick, he voluntarily enlisted in the British Army in 1915 when he was aged just 17. Posted to the Mesopotamian front during World War I, his military career was not an illustrious one and he was involved in several minor scrapes with authority. He was appointed bombardier (corporal) in March 1916, but, at his own request, relinquished this rank two months later. This move seems surprising in the context of his later life when he proved himself more than comfortable in a leadership role. It was, however, in Mesopotamia he belatedly learned of the Easter Rising in Dublin which he subsequently described as a "rude awakening", having known almost nothing previously about Irish history. According to Meda Ryan in her book *Tom Barry - Irish Freedom Fighter*, this was a turning point in his life with Barry later stating "It put me thinking. What the hell was I doing in the British Army. It's with the Irish I should be."

Certainly, his action of joining the army would eventually create one of the ironies of Barry's life. When the Soloheadbeg Ambush on January 21, 1919 - which was led by IRA volunteers Séamus Robinson, Seán Treacy and Dan Breen - instigated the War of Independence (although there are some who dispute this, claiming that it was just one incident in a long and inevitable slide into war) Barry was, ironic as it may seem, a serving soldier of the British Army. He could - in theory at least - have been ordered to help suppress this growing insurrection in West Tipperary.

Discharged from the army in April 1919, he returned to a vastly different Ireland from the one he had departed. Ireland was having yet another of its periodic identity crises as the old certainties supplied by the moderate Irish Parliamentary Party were confined to the dustbin of history. In December 1918, the first general election in over eight years was the initial one where all women over the age of 30, and all men over the age of 21, could vote, which extended the size of the electorate threefold. Previously, females and most working-class men had been denied a vote. This extended suffrage brought the Labour Party to the forefront of politics in Britain and also helped Sinn Fein sweep to victory as a new and radical political force in Ireland. As an avowed Irexit party, long before the term was coined, Sinn Fein believed the protection of native industry from international competition in an independent Ireland would raise all economic boats.

Ironically, this was also the election that copper-fastened the partition of Ireland. Refusing to take their seats in the British House of Commons, the newly elected Sinn Fein MPs assembled at an alternative Irish Parliament in Dublin's Mansion House, that they titled the Dáil. Unsurprisingly, the elected Unionists MPs (mostly from the northeast of the country) continued to sit in the British House of Commons; for the first time the partition of Ireland became a political reality. The partition of Ireland was then copper-fastened when a separate parliament for north-eastern six counties came into being in June 1921.

Despite returning to a nation brimming with revolutionary fervour and captivating dreams of a new and better Ireland, Barry showed little immediate interest in the atmosphere of seismic change that was sweeping the country. With the idea of an independent Irish republic now disinterred from the era of the Fenians and the Irish War of Independence slowly gathering pace, Barry seems, initially at least, to have taken pride in his military record while demonstrating little interest in being "with the Irish". As evidence, he was happy to hoist a union flag in Bandon to mark the 1919 anniversary of the ending of World War I. Soon after, while studying commerce in Cork City he came, however, into the gravitational field of the Hales brothers, who came from a radically republican family in West Cork and introduced him to Republican ideals.

It was the torture of IRA prisoners by the British Army's Essex Regiment – particularly of volunteers Tom Hales and Patrick Harte, with the latter suffering irreversible brain damage – that was apparently the final catalyst for Barry that brought an abrupt change of heart. Afterwards, Barry carried a deep personal animosity against Major Arthur Percival of the Essex Regiment whom he regarded as, at least indirectly, responsible for these tortures. Later, he described Percival as "easily the most viciously anti-Irish of all serving British officers". Over 20 years on, Barry would surely have allowed himself a wry smile when he learned that, on another island far away, Percival had made himself infamous as the general who surrendered Singapore and 80 thousand British troops to a much lesser force of Japanese in 1942.

After some difficulty convincing a sceptical leadership of the bona fides of a man who was the son of an RIC sergeant and had spent almost four years in the British Army, Barry was eventually allowed join the 3rd West Cork Brigade IRA at a time when its organisation structure was changing. He had now placed himself on the right side of history where he could surf the new tide of radical republicanism that was sweeping all before it. Under a directive from Michael Collins, the IRA units were instructed to organise flying columns in September 1920. These would consist of fulltime and highly mobile units that were tasked to carry out hit-and-run raids. Barry's military experience immediately made him an ideal candidate for this operation.

His first military engagement was at Toureen on the main Cork Bandon Road where he commanded a section of the volunteers.

Soldiers from the Essex Regiment were ambushed and according to Barry, five were killed and four were wounded with no casualties among the IRA volunteers. Six soldiers who were not hurt surrendered. They were released along with the wounded and returned to their barracks

After drifting rather listlessly through life, it seemed Barry had finally found his tribe. Soon after Toureen, he was made commander of the Brigades flying column. Handpicking those he wanted to serve in the column, Barry then moulded these young men, who had no previous experience of combat, into a fearsome fighting unit. The rolling hills of West Cork facilitated the stealthy movement of the flying column. It also made ideal ambush territory with much of the road system overlooked by high ground. Barry quickly became adept at using both these advantages to the full and in a short time had achieved a situation where the British writ no longer ran in West Cork.

The 23-year-old Barry then sprang to international prominence at Kilmichael, south of Macroom, Co. Cork, on November 28th. As dusk fell on this lonesome road, 36 volunteers under his command ambushed and annihilating a patrol of 17 Auxiliaries in controversial and much disputed circumstances. Barry afterwards claimed a false surrender on the British side was used as an opportunity to kill IRA volunteers Pat Deasy and Jim Sullivan. This he argued, meant the flying column was obliged to resume firing until there was no further resistance. Whatever the reason, Kilmichael certainly turned out a fight to the finish with no prisoners taken. In a graphic description of the aftermath of the ambush, Barry displays a remarkable ability to remain detached from the situation. In his book, *Guerilla Days in Ireland*, he vividly describes the lorries of the auxiliaries burning in the cold night air and he marching his men back and forth between the corpses in order to restore discipline after the trauma of the ambush.

The Auxiliary Division was a well-paid paramilitary unit made up of former British Army officers. They were brought to Ireland to conduct counter insurgency at a time when large numbers of the Royal Irish Constabulary were resigning their posts. Standing out in rural Ireland because of their seemingly incomprehensible accents, they immediately transformed the war into an Anglo-Irish conflict, soon becoming almost universally reviled by the local population because of their atrocities against the civilians. Most notable was the burning of Cork City, which proved counterproductive and just stiffened the resolve of the Irish people. The result was that Barry's success, against what were seen locally as oppressive and foreign forces, inevitably raised him to an almost cult status in Co. Cork.

Subsequent to Kilmichael, Barry collapsed. Diagnosed with a displaced heart - he had previously been found to have a "Disordered Action of the Heart" while serving in the British army - he spent almost a month being covertly cared for by sympathetic nuns in Cork's Mercy Home. Here, he was informed of a pastoral letter from the Bishop of Cork, Daniel Coholan, declaring that any Catholic taking part in an ambush was a murderer and would be excommunicated from the Church. Undaunted by this unwelcome intervention, he discharged himself from the hospital and was quickly back to his old ways, harassing crown forces and loyalist sympathisers with unrelenting tenacity. He was now Cork's most wanted man. When information was received that he had headquartered the Flying Column near the appropriately titled village of Crossbarry, a major encircling operation, involving over 1,000 British troops, began.

Showing his credentials as a first order military strategist, Barry immediately did the unexpected: counter-attacking a section of the surrounding line of soldiers that had become detached from the main force. Breaking through the encirclement, he left behind at least ten dead British soldiers for the loss of three volunteers. The action at Crossbarry acted as a considerable blow to British morale as it was to be the first and only time in the Irish War of Independence that crown forces were defeated in what amounted to conventional battle.

Subsequent to Crossbarry, ever-increasing numbers of British troops were poured into West Cork to the extent that active IRA volunteers were outnumbered 40 to 1. At the end of May, a second attempt was made to destroy Barry's forces. Thousands of troops drawn from as far away as Kildare pursued the Flying Column relentlessly west and south and by early June, they were compressed into a tiny corner of the south-west. This time there was to be no escape.

Seemingly undaunted by events, Barry led his men up the isolated Coomhoola Valley towards a high pass known locally as the Priest's Leap. He had now entered the wild and trackless range of mountains which form a geographic rampart dividing the counties of Cork and Kerry. If Barry were to continue through the mountains he would, of course, fall into the hands of blockading British troops to the west, but once again he did the unexpected. He was aware that to the east lay the valley of Gougane Barra containing an ancient monastic site founded by St Finbarr, patron saint of Co. Cork, since he had already conducted military training at this isolated location. If the Flying Column could reach this sanctuary, they would be outside the British blockade on the Keimaneigh Pass and relatively safe. The problem was, however, that to gain Gougane Barra, the volunteers would first have to descend into the Coomroe Valley, which is referred to by Barry as Deepvalley Desmond. To achieve this, it would be necessary to climb down 300m cliffs.

In anticipation of this descent, local IRA Commander, Captain Din Cronin, was tasked to collect every piece of rope in the Coomhoola Valley. Then, after nightfall, Barry moved his men onto the isolated Shehy Mountains under the guidance of local man, Murty Cronin. The account in his book *Guerilla Days in Ireland* (sic) vividly describes a nightmarish march of many hours in thick darkness, often sinking knee deep in boggy ground while clinging to the rope for security. "Without this man's help [Murty Cronin] men would have floundered to their deaths in the deep holes on either side, but eventually he led us all safely to the top of Deepvalley Desmond, beneath which lay lonely Gougane Barra."

When I arrived to follow in the footsteps of Tom Barry, it was a benign summer day with just a few puffy clouds in the sky. The first thought to strike me was how the austerely beautiful hills of West Cork would make ideal terrain in which to wage a guerrilla war; Barry certainly had the terrain on his side.

Starting amid the bewitching bleakness of the Borlin Valley at Upper Gowlane Bridge, which was the departure point for the volunteers, I followed a stream east and then northeast tagging an ancient mass path until the gurgling waters eventually petered out. Continuing in the same direction through a shallow col amid undulating but relatively unchallenging moorland terrain, it struck me that Barry's description of the trek might just be a tiny bit like purple prose; little evidence existed of the deep holes on either side where the men would have floundered to their deaths.

But, of course, I was viewing the terrain from the point of view of an experienced hillwalker operating in perfect conditions during daylight hours while the volunteers were crossing unknown and frightening terrain in the hours of darkness which would inevitably play tricks with perception. Unable to properly see the terrain around, it is likely the volunteer's brains would have worked overtime to fill in details that realised their deepest fears.

Eventually, the column reached the rim of the great cliffs above Coomroe, where without guidance the men would certainly fall to their deaths. Cronin, however, knew the one weakness in the stout ramparts guarding the valley below, a descent route known locally as Poll. This consists of a steep, rocky defile that narrows at one point into a treacherous gully before offering access to Coomroe. It was their only feasible escape route into Gougane Barra. Having descended Poll several times myself, I have discovered to my cost that, even in daylight, it is a steep, wet, knee-twisting gully where even experienced hill-walkers must exercise great diligence. For the column descending in darkness it must have been epic, with the constant danger of falling or being hit by rocks displaced by those above. In the claustrophobic confines of Poll, history suddenly comes to life, I feel as if I can almost hear the heavy breathing of the men as they scrambled and slithered towards safety. Barry vividly describes volunteers slithering downwards with the aid of stretched-out rifles and a number of ropes which had been tied together to form a single line by Murty Cronin.

An hour later, "bruised and wrenched" but without serious injury, they reached the valley floor of Coomroe from where it was just an easy walk to Gougane Barra and the hospitality provided by Bridget Cronin in the local hotel. Feeding and billeting 100 hungry men is no mean feat, but this mammoth task didn't prove a problem as the ladies of the local Cumann na mBan (women's volunteers organisation, IRA) had already collected food and blankets from the surrounding valleys.

According to Barry's description from *Guerilla Days in Ireland*, Gougane Barra is "probably the best defensive fighting country in Ireland. Only a small, twisting, easily-defended rough road led to our billet area while behind us stretched miles and miles of roadless mountain land well covered with bracken and dotted with large rocks across the hills to the Kerry valley."

A defensive battle wasn't, however, required, as the next day frustrated British forces abandoned the roundup and returned forlornly to barracks. Shortly afterwards Barry led his column triumphantly out of Gougane Barra. The Scarlet Pimpernel of West Cork had escaped once again.

Meanwhile, public opinion in Britain and particularly the United States had turned against the brutal way the war in Ireland was being conducted. Atrocities might be quietly ignored at far-flung corners of the empire, but here they were happening within the United

Kingdom. Soon British authorities were in secret negotiations with Sinn Fein. The resultant Truce not only concluded the War of Independence, but also dropped a curtain on Tom Barry's brief but highly successful epoch as a guerrilla fighter, who had successfully resisted the might of the British Empire. For the previous eight months, the requirements of the situation, from the Republican point of view, had perfectly matched Barry's deeply held convictions and expansive skill set. These circumstances never recurred. While rebellion, by its nature, is inspirational, it also releases unpredictable forces that invariably create instability. In the case of Ireland, it led to an unforeseen but extremely bitter civil war.

Like most of the IRA volunteers, Barry disagreed with the Treaty that followed upon the Truce. He took the anti-Treaty side in the subsequent Civil War, which opposed the partitioning of Ireland and even advocated renewing the conflict with an attack on the remaining British forces in Ireland. Ironically, he soon became what he had never been previously during the fight for of independence - a prisoner of war. Captured in 1922 trying to join a Republican garrison in the Dublin Four Courts - while disguised as a nurse - he became the first detainee of the conflict. Initially gaoled in Dublin's Mountjoy and Kilmainham, he was later transferred to Gormanstown Internment Camp, Co. Meath. Unsurprisingly perhaps, he soon escaped, thus appearing to foil plans for his execution.

Afterwards, he made his way back to his old stomping ground among the hills of West Cork. From this base, he fought determinedly for the Republican cause as leader of 200 West Cork Republicans and was the only anti-treaty commander to carry the fight to the Free State Army. Short of arms and supplies and with his forces vastly outnumbered and fighting an enemy already well experienced with guerrilla warfare, it is not surprising that Barry never managed to replicate the successes he enjoyed when in combat with British forces. Towards the end of the Civil War he came to realise

the pointlessness of it all and became a voice urging the discontinu-
ation of the fruitless "brother on brother" fighting.

After formal hostilities ended in 1923, it would appear that Barry
never again found his tribe. He remained committed to physical force
to achieve the unification of Ireland, but from this point on he was
a marginal, if articulate, proponent of republicanism. In 1949, Barry
returned to the limelight when he published his memoirs of the War of
Independence under the title *Guerilla Days in Ireland*. Not as fluently
written as other accounts of the period, such as the highly readable *On
Another Man's Wound* by Ernie O'Malley, and straying sometimes into
self-righteousness, Guerilla Days is, nevertheless, regarded as a classic.
It is a definitive account of the tactics employed in irregular warfare,
which is now required reading for military personnel seeking a guide
to a better understanding of guerrilla strategies. Over 60 years after
its publication, the book still resonated and was adopted for the stage
before playing to full houses across Ireland.

Having tried to find out as much as possible about Tom Barry's
life and followed in his footsteps around west Cork, I concluded this
was a man who could be ruthless and pitiless when he felt he had
to be. He was particularly merciless towards those he regarded as
British collaborators and this has made him a controversial figure
among historians. He was, however, also a person of unshakeable
principle and seems, on the surface at least, to have lacked any
form of self-doubt. These attributes were, very likely, factors in his
under-achievement later in life, for his one Shakespearian character
flaw appears to have been an inability to compromise. After the Civil
War ended, Barry entrenched himself on the wrong side of history
and soon drifted far from the levers of political power that were now
held by many of his more compliant former associates in the new
Ireland. Continuing to espouse the use of physical force to bring
about a united Ireland, he was subsequently jailed by a government
that was led by his former anti-treaty comrade, Éamon de Valera.

Afterwards, he became a somewhat peripatetic figure around which it is difficult to from a coherent narrative. Drifting between revolutionary violence and sorties into constitutional politics when he stood unsuccessfully for elected office in his native Cork, he never appeared to find his niche. With the benefit of hindsight, this seems something of a pity. Had he managed to accommodate the compromises which so many of his less gifted comrades-in-arms achieved, his leadership talents and undoubted charisma could surely have made a valuable contribution to the fledgling state.

# CHAPTER 9

# The Unwavering Republican

On April 9th 1923, Tom Taylor, a captain in the Irish Free State Army based in Clogheen, Co. Tipperary, received orders from his Commanding Officer, Major General John Prout, who was based in Clonmel. He was to proceed at daybreak with a detachment of soldiers to the village of Newcastle, which lay in the eastern shadow of the Knockmealdown Mountains. In his order, Prout, who had served in the American Army during World War I, specified that he had reliable information that "important Irregular Leaders [Republicans, who rejected the partition of Ireland] are at present in South Tipperary or Waterford". His intention was to surround the area and capture the enemy as stated in his order to Taylor. "At dawn you will drive out from Newcastle in a south-easterly direction with your troops in well extended formation. Search all farmyards and other likely places across the Knockmealdown Mountains and foothills holding a well extended line across the mountain, Ballymacarbry and Melleray left and right respectively, when you will link up with a column from Dungarvan operating in a north-westerly direction."

The Irish Civil War was in its final month and Lieutenant Larry Clancy was a Free State army officer based in Clogheen. With Captain Taylor he was tasked with routing Republican forces based in the area. According to his account, later published in the *Evening Herald* newspaper, his soldiers arrived at Goatenbridge near Newcastle around daybreak. Here, a second-class road leads towards the foot of the Knockmealdowns. Clancy led a detachment of troops up this minor road, while aware that another contingent of Free State soldiers was moving towards the area from the opposite direction, using the road from the south. As they moved uphill a burst of firing came from the right, a few hundred yards in front of the Free State soldiers.

Not sure if this was "friendly fire" from other army units, Clancy ordered the men to take cover and ran to a nearby rock with binoculars to scan the hillside. About 400 yards in front, he was surprised to see a group of men "daringly standing on rocks while wearing black overcoats and hats and firing from Peters and Parabellum autos with arms out-stretched. I then knew they were Republicans and I gave the range at four fifty yards" recalled Clancy. "We fired off five rounds and I saw them jumping off the rocks before the bullets ceased to whiz around us and then using my glasses, I saw them running down the hill towards the skyline. I then observed a man fall forward and remain there. All stopped and two of the group turned back to him and began to drag him on his back away up the hill towards the remainder who were going away hesitatingly. I shouted 'we have got one of them, fire again and don't let them take him'. At that moment I saw the two men who were dragging the body stand for a few moments, then turn and run away, leaving the wounded man behind lying on the hillside."

Delayed when accidentally fired on by another detachment of Free State soldiers, Clancy and his men eventually reached the fallen Republican. "When we got near to where the man was lying on his back with a topcoat folded under his head, one of our men said. 'We have Dev' [Éamon de Valera, President of the Republic who, like Lynch, was also tall and bespectacled]. But I knew Mr de Valera by sight, so I said 'No, it's not Dev, who are you?' and the man answered, 'I'm Liam Lynch, get me a priest and a doctor, I'm dying'." recalled Clancy.

Liam Lynch was one of seven children born in 1893 to Jeremiah Lynch and Mary Lynch, (neé Kelly) who had a small farm in the townland of Barnagurraha, Co. Limerick. Although the family had a tradition of political activism, Lynch's formative years were relatively tranquil ones in Irish history. Economic circumstances had improved immeasurably in the half-decade since the Great Famine and the land of Ireland was gradually being returned to Irish farmers by a succession of Land Acts. The extension of voting rights to about half the male population and the introduction of secret ballots in 1872 brought about a profound change to the political landscape. Unlike the Scottish and Welsh MPs, who tended to become members of the two main parties in the British House of Commons, most of the MPs from Ireland came together within the new and highly influential Irish Parliamentary Party. They then began actively campaigning towards home rule for Ireland. With self-government now a strong possibility, constitutional politics appeared the way ahead and the thought of revolution was far from the minds of all but a marginal few. After many turbulent centuries, Ireland finally seemed to be at ease with itself.

When I visited Lynch's birthplace, it was immediately apparent that this is a setting where a living would be hard-won by tenant farmers from an unforgiving mountainside. Barnagurraha is a place of small, sloping fields clinging to the western slopes of the Galtee Mountains with the great peaks of Templehill and Lyrragappul towering above. Now abandoned, the buildings of the former Lynch farmstead are still apparent, located about 1km north of the village of Anglesboro. By any standards, Barnagurrah is an isolated upland and immediately appears the sort of place likely to breed those with a no-nonsense streak of rugged individualism and a strong sense of historic grievance. Certainly, the local people have not forgotten their most famous son. A tribute to his memory in the form of a large Celtic Cross was erected in 1978 on the opposite side of the road to where he lived.

Lynch attended Anglesboro National School for a period of 12 years. Described by his teacher as a "mild gentle boy of above average intelligence" he commenced work, in 1910, as an apprentice to the O'Neill hardware business in nearby Mitchelstown. Although he joined the Gaelic League and the Ancient Order of Hibernians, there was little to suggest a republican outlook and initially, at least, he was a supporter – like most Irish people at the time - of the moderate Irish Parliamentary Party. Unlike his compatriot, Tom Barry, he did not heed the urging of IPP leader, John Redmond, to join the British Army and fight for the cause of small nations in World War I. With no intention of joining the armed forces of his majesty, he instead took up a position in 1915 at Barry's Timber Merchants in Fermoy. Later, he absented himself from work for a period in 1918 when conscription into the British Army was being threatened upon Irish men.

In Fermoy, he met local woman Bridie Keyes when both were studying the Irish language. They soon became engaged and agreed that they would eventually get married. A life of comfortable conformity appeared to beckon but, almost unnoticed, underlying seismic pressures were building up in society that were soon to implode like an overstressed dam. As with Tom Barry, a single act of brutality would bring about a totally changed mindset. The moment of epiphany came for Lynch when, in 1916, he witnessed a blood stained Republican named Tom Kent being dragged through the streets following his arrest by the Royal Irish Constabulary. Radicalised in his outlook, he joined the Irish Volunteers, who were no longer satisfied with just home rule for Ireland but were now committed to a 32 county independent republic. In those days nobody worried about the economic consequences of exiting the UK or the nature of the future relationship with Great Britain. Instead, the tide of events had begun creeping remorselessly towards war.

Lynch's formidable organisational skills quickly ensured that by the start of the War of Independence in 1919, he was commander of the No 2, Cork Brigade. Unsurprisingly, plans for marriage were now put on hold. Instead, the new commander organised the first military action against British soldiers since the 1916 Rising. In September, a party of 15 British soldiers was attacked by Lynch's men in the Cork town of Fermoy. The soldiers were overpowered, their rifles were taken and one of their number was killed in the action.

Another notable action by Lynch was the capture of Major General Lucas, while he was fishing on the River Blackwater outside Fermoy. He was the most senior British Army officer to fall into the hands of the IRA. When he finally escaped after over four weeks in captivity, Lucas declared he had been treated as "a gentleman by gentlemen".

In 1920, Lynch spent some time in Dublin where he so impressed the Volunteer leader, Michael Collins, that he was offered the post of Deputy Chief of Staff. Lynch politely declined this offer, preferring to return to his men in Cork. Once back in Mallow, he joined with fellow Republican, Ernie O'Malley, to command the only IRA force to capture a British Army barracks and escaped with a large haul of weapons. He organised two further successful ambushes of British troops that year and followed these in 1921 with an attack on British soldiers near Millstreet, Co. Cork. In April, the IRA was re-organised into divisions and Lynch became commander of the entire 1st Southern Division, a position he held until the July 1921 truce with British forces. Fearing a rapid return to hostilities, Lynch did not, like many other IRA leaders, use the period to get married. He remained politically active and, like most IRA men, opposed the Anglo-Irish Treaty of December 6th, which proposed the partition of Ireland.

Initially regarded as a moderate, he sought desperately to avoid civil war. As so often happens in a Shakespearian tragedy, events took on a momentum of their own, without anybody wanting this to happen. The wisdom of Solomon would have been required to prevent the gathering clouds of conflict, but none such was available.

Soon both sides were on a war footing, with the anti-treaty officers electing Lynch Chief of Staff of the Irish Republican Army.

Lynch was initially opposed to the occupation of the Dublin Four Courts and other public buildings in the capital city by Republicans. When the Free State forces, who had accepted the Treaty with Britain, attacked these buildings, he immediately left a largely hostile Dublin and headed south. Arrested en route, he was released on the apparent understanding he would try to stop the fighting. This decision probably did much to actually prolong the conflict.

Returned to his stronghold in the south of Ireland he instead created a "Munster Republic" that denied the legitimacy of the Irish Free State. Lynch was later criticized by those who suggested his one chance of outright victory was an immediate assault on Dublin before the Free State Government had time to organise and obtain supplies from the British. The reason he hesitated may, however, have been the fact that there were still thousands of British soldiers in Ireland. In the eventuality of an attack on Dublin, these would likely have come out on the pro-treaty side making outright victory for the republicans an impossibility.

Short on weapons, ammunition, and men, Lynch refused to go on the attack and instead mounted a defensive campaign. With generous British support in terms of rifles, machine guns and artillery, the Free State Army was soon on the offensive. Lynch was outflanked by a seaborne landing of Free State soldiers to his rear, which was led by his former comrade in the War of Independence, Major General Emmet Dalton. Dalton captured Cork City and soon after drove the Republicans from all the major towns in their Munster stronghold. Lynch then ordered his forces to form flying columns (small mobile units) and fight a guerrilla campaign as had been the case when they fought in the War of Independence against the British.

This departure did not, however, pay dividends as their opponents were well-versed in the use of such tactics. Outnumbered and hampered by lack of supplies, declining public support and the vehement opposition of the Catholic Hierarchy, the Republican forces soon found themselves unable to mount an effective campaign against the Free State Army.

Early in 1923, the position had become increasingly desperate for the Republican forces. Withdrawn into remote and mountainous areas where their most secure support base lay, there was little they could do beyond mounting attacks on public infrastructure and burning the homes of government and unionist supporters. The war had now degenerated into an ugly campaign of atrocities followed by inevitable reprisals, with both sides clearly demonstrating they could match, if not exceed, the British in terms of the savagery of their actions. By the spring of 1923, the Republican leadership was, to all intents and purposes, "on the run" from the Free State Army with Lynch coming under increasing pressure from some of his fellow IRA officers to call a cease-fire.

With the military situation now apparently hopeless, the available members of the Anti-Treaty IRA Army Executive were called to a meeting in the home of James Cullinane which lay at Bleantasour in the shadow of the Monavullagh Mountains, Co. Waterford. Along with Lynch, other prominent Republicans to attend included: Austin Stack, Tom Barry, Frank Aiken and Sean MacSwiney, (brother of famous Republican hunger striker, Terence MacSwiney).

Movements by Free State soldiers in this area meant that the meeting was constantly interrupted and soon had to be switched to the home of John Wall. This house, which has since been demolished, lay deep into the Comeragh Mountains and on the lower slopes of Knockanaffrin in the Nire Valley of Co. Waterford. The location had the advantage of offering a perfect emergency escape along an ancient trade route through Comeragh Mountain Gap, which lay directly to the west. It was then, and still is, an extremely remote location and, with only one narrow road serving it, made for an ideal defensive position. With protection provided by the local company of the IRA, the meeting reconvened here on March 25th. An old man I once met while walking in the Nire told me that even with this protection, the meeting had to be adjourned several times because of movements by Free State soldiers in the area.

The future Irish Taoiseach (Prime Minister), Éamon de Valera, made the long and difficult journey to the meeting but was initially denied admission as he was, by this time, considered a non-military man. Forced to sit forlornly in the kitchen for a time, while his position was discussed, he was eventually admitted and allowed speak in support of ending the conflict, but was not permitted to vote on the issue.

Several members of the Executive, including the influential Tom Barry also favoured ending the Civil War. Apparently embittered by the conduct of the fighting on behalf of the Free State, Lynch opposed ending the war and carried a division with a majority of one. It was, however, agreed to reconvene the meeting for a further discussion of options in the West Waterford village of Araglin, on April 10th.

Moving from one safe house to another, Lynch managed to stay ahead of the Free State army. At Easter, he arranged a brief meeting with his girlfriend, Bridie Keyes, at Graigvalla, Co. Waterford – this would be their last time together as they were never destined to meet again in this life. After saying goodbye, Lynch travelled by a circuitous route through the Comeragh Mountains and eventually arrived at Goatenbridge, in the shadow of the Knockmealdown Mountains. Here, he learned of movements by Free State troops in the Araglin area and relocated the executive meeting to Goatenbridge. Would he have agreed to end the Civil War at this meeting? We will never know for certain, but with the IRA no longer able to secure even the assembly of its own Executive, it must have been increasingly clear to Lynch the conflict could not now be won. Certainly, some memos scribbled casually in his notebook at this time suggest he was considering bringing an end to hostilities.

The meeting did not, however, take place. Reports that a column of Free State soldiers was moving out from Clogheen forced Lynch and other members of the Executive to move during the night to the Houlihan home - the remotest house on the mountainside. The IRA men were settling down for a cup of tea at 8 am when a sentry came to tell them that a column of soldiers was heading directly for them. One crucial weakness to their position would now become apparent; a minor road from the south gave easy access to the mountain above them. In an attempt to escape, Lynch and his companions rushed towards Crohan West Mountain, but Free State soldiers coming from this road appeared over a nearby crest. Initially, the republicans were able to use the cover of a riverbed to move upwards. Such mountain features tend to disappear with height and soon they had no choice but to cross open ground. The pursuing soldiers fired at the fleeing group while the Republicans shot back ineffectively with revolvers.

When I arrived to check out the lie of the land where Lynch died, it was immediately clear that the location of the Houlihan homestead, which was situated at the end of a long dogleg lane that runs for over 2 km, lacked little for remoteness. It was, however, difficult to get an impression of the landscape as it was in Lynch's time, since the Knockmealdowns have been generously planted with commercial timber during the intervening years. In the time of Lynch, the area would have been completely bare and comparable to what the Sugarloaf Mountain at the Vee Gap looks like today. Since no planting has taken place on the upper slopes of the Sugarloaf, humans on its slopes stand out clearly against the heathery background.

Almost nothing remains of the Houlihan home, but the deep glen up which the men escaped is immediately obvious. Following it tortuously uphill, I eventually came to where the stream rose sharply out of the glen to gain open mountainside. It was here, according to

Maurice Toomey, who accompanied Lynch on the attempted escape, that the men exchanged the first shots of the engagement with the Free State Army. Struggling with difficulty upwards out of the glen, I found the river continues uphill in a much narrower but still reasonably deep ravine. As I walked up through the centre of the stream, I was confident I would have been well out of the sight for any snipers over 400 yards away. There is, however, one fatal flaw in their escape plans that the IRA fugitives would hardly have had time to consider. As one ascends a mountain, soil depth generally becomes thinner; a stream running along the bedrock will most likely be just below the surface and so provide little cover. And so, it came to pass that as I reached a forest roadway running at right angles to the stream, the ravine - to what must have been the consternation of the fugitives - suddenly disappeared. In the remaining few hundred metres uphill, the nascent stream affords no protection whatsoever.

Twomey's account of events accurately matches what I observed. "We dashed on again up the mountain, a shallow riverbed affording us cover for about 250 yards. When we reached the end of the riverbed, we had to retreat up a bare coverless shoulder of mountain." A later description from Frank Aiken in a letter to Fr Tom Lynch, brother of Liam, gives another indication of the terrain at this time when he stated "The fight took place on mountain as bare as a billiard table."

The IRA men had progressed about 1km uphill from the Houlihan farmhouse when a single shot rang out; Lynch fell forward, while crying "My God! I'm hit, lads!" Two members of his party, Bill Quirke and Sean Hyde, began dragging their stricken leader uphill, with one reciting an Act of Contrition in his ear. Lynch begged his companions several times to leave him until they saw the futility of what they were attempting and the added pain being caused and left him down on the mountainside. Just delaying long enough to pick up his gun and some vital Republican documents, they then made their escape across the mountain.

Lynch was a bitter and deadly opponent of those who accepted the Treaty with Britain and had just recently described the Free State Government as a Junta and the Dáil as "its so-called parliament". Despite this, the Free State soldiers made every effort to save the badly wounded Lynch. Laboriously they carried their former comrade using an improvised stretcher on the long journey down the mountainside. He was then loaded onto a haycart and carried to Nugent's Pub in Newcastle village, where he was laid on a sofa and given medical treatment and spiritual comfort.

According to a statement later made by Lieutenant Clancy, he told Lynch he had lost 2 brothers in the War of Independence. Lynch then grasped the lieutenant's hand and spoke with difficulty saying "God pray for me. All this is a pity. It should never have happened. I am glad now I am going from it all, Poor Ireland. Poor Ireland." In a bitter-sweet moment, he then presented Clancy with his silver pen as a poignant symbol of respect for the erstwhile comrades he had served with in the War of Independence. Soon after, he was transferred by ambulance to Clonmel Hospital where he succumbed to his wounds. He was just 29 years of age.

Lynch was unlucky to expire from a single shot in the final weeks of the Civil War when escape seemed more probable. He died at a time when the Irish Republican movement was at its lowest ebb with little apparent future. Yet, within ten years, Éamon de Valera would lead many of Lynch's former comrades into government of the Irish Free State. Had he survived would Lynch have been among them? No one will ever know if his radical outlook would have allowed him join the government of a partitioned Ireland. But, as a deep thinker with natural leadership abilities and a distinguished active service record where he invariably conducted himself with the highest standards as a soldier, it is difficult to imagine that a place in Government would not have been available to him had he so chosen. The great tragedy of the Irish Civil War was undoubtedly the improbable single shots from distance that killed both Lynch and Michael Collins.

Two days later, at Kilcrumper Cemetery, near Fermoy, Co. Cork, Lynch was buried. By his own request, he was laid beside fellow Republican, Michael Fitzgerald, who died on hunger strike in 1920, while in British custody. This event marked the effective end of the Civil War. On April 20th, at a Republican hideout known as "Kathmandu" near Mullinahone, Co. Tipperary, Frank Aiken, who would later go on to a stellar career in Irish politics, was elected IRA Chief of Staff. A ceasefire on behalf of the anti-treaty forces followed soon afterwards with Aiken ordering the IRA to dump arms rather than surrender. The most shameful period in Irish history had finally come to an end.

Ireland's strong consciousness of its history has, however, ensured that Lynch has not been forgotten. Just over a decade later, local Republicans carried up the stone on donkeys for a monument to Lynch at the site where he had been shot. The result is a striking 20m edifice that now bears testament to Lynch's unrealised dreams. The monument is based on the Irish round towers of the early Christian period that are commonly associated with monastic settlements at this time. On April 7th, 1935, Maurice Twomey returned to Crohan Mountain, while still a fugitive, and unveiled the memorial with the attendance being estimated at 15,000. The surrounding bronze wolfhounds, which were added in 1996, are the work of sculptor Pauline O'Connell and a clear attempt to link Lynch to Ireland's heroic past.

Reflecting on Lynch's turbulent life in the course of my research, I came to the conclusion that he was at heart a decent man brutalised, like many others, by war. Without the catalyst of a pitiless conflict, it is likely he would have lived a conformist, productive but unremarkable life and would almost certainly have been considered a good neighbour. His impeccably correct treatment of his prisoner

Major General Lucas appears to bear out his basic decency. But, as is often the case with such men who believe strongly in equality and justice, they easily become radicalised by witnessing an act of brutality they could never countenance doing themselves. This commonly appears to raise an uncontrollable anger deep within, which in the case of Lynch appeared to have reached a crescendo of hatred against his former comrades during the Civil War. In Shakespearian parlance, he would probably be viewed as a tragic victim of the overwhelming social forces that were unleashed during his lifetime.

Certainly, he has not been forgotten. Almost a century after his death, considerable numbers of people still make the pilgrimage up Crohan Mountain each July. In memory of Lynch, they stand reverently at the site where a man they never knew died while vainly attempting to achieve that in which he passionately believed – an independent 32 county Irish republic.

# CHAPTER 10

# The Ancient Journey

" **A**s you walk you will be going not only on a spiritual pilgrimage, but on a cultural and historical journey that will take you down through the ages also. And if you take it upon yourself to enter fully into these experiences, this should bring about the change of heart and insight of mind which is essential to a pilgrim's progress." With these uplifting words from Father Frank Fahey in the beautifully restored church of Ballintubber Abbey we are inducted into the pilgrim experience. Requested not to complain and to include the stranger in our group as we journey, we are told that pilgrimage consists of five elements: faith, penance, community, change of heart and final celebration. Then, having been requested to first light a candle in the Abbey Church before setting out, we are released to the considerable challenge of Ireland's most renowned penitential path.

I am in Mayo to explore what meaning pilgrimage holds in 21st Century Ireland by completing the ancient 35km pilgrim path leading from Ballintubber Abbey to Croagh Patrick, which is Ireland's oldest pilgrim trail. It is also one of Europe's most ancient penitential routes, long predating the much more youthful, but presently better known, Spanish Camino. To facilitate this journey, I join a group about to finish the full Irish pilgrim journey which requires completion of 120km on five medieval penitential paths. Having finished Cnoc na dTobar and Cosáin na Naomh, in Co. Kerry along with St Finbarr's Pilgrim Path, Co. Cork and St Kevin's Way, Co. Wicklow, the final requirement for the group is the ancient Tóchar Phádraig to the mystical mountain of Croagh Patrick. As I arrive, everyone is in high spirits as they look forward to the journey's end and receiving their Teastas (completion certificate) afterwards.

Ballintubber Abbey has a long and turbulent history. Situated on the shores of Lough Carra, the Abbey was built by Cathal O'Connor, King of Connacht, in 1216 for the Augustinian Canons Regular. The only church in Ireland that was founded by an Irish King, it has been continually in use ever since. In the medieval period, it became an important overnight stop for pilgrims making their way along the Tóchar to Croagh Patrick.

The Abbey was located in a Gaelic controlled part of Ireland and so was out of reach of the general monastic dissolution by Henry VIII. After the fall of Gaelic Ireland, however, its land holdings were confiscated by James I in 1603. The Abbey was then taken over by the Augustinian friars, who as a mendicant order did not require land. Their time in the abbey was short-lived, however. Most of the buildings were burned by Cromwellian soldiers in the mid-17th Century, but the church escaped total destruction and has continued unbroken as a place of worship throughout the intervening centuries.

Before the off, I make time to visit the grave of the notorious priest hunter Seán na Sagart, which lies in the abbey grounds. In early Penal times, Catholic priests and bishops had, in common with wolves, a price on their heads. This sometimes proved an irresistible temptation for poor people who perceived easy money. It is said that Seán, whose name was John Malowney, was responsible for the capture of a number of priests and then claiming the price on their heads. Stabbed to death by a local man while trying to detain a priest, his body was thrown into a lake by local people. The priest whom Sean had been trying to detain ordered, however, that the body be taken from the lake and given a Christian burial. Seán was then buried in Ballintubber, but in a mark of disrespect, he was faced north so that he would never see the rising sun. A local tradition holds that an ash tree grew up soon and split his grave in two. This part of the story certainly holds true for, sure enough, a large ash tree has grown up from the grave and split the great concrete slab above the tomb.

Then it's time for the off, but before we set out there is a reminder that early Tóchar pilgrimages were undertaken without such self-indulgent fripperies as boots. Passing the remains of foot baths, we are reminded by Fr Fahey that penitents bathed here on their return after their barefoot walk to and from Croagh Patrick.

Released into a landscape drenched in history and abounding with myth-making potential, we soon find ourselves tramping some of the original stones of the ancient path still visible beneath out feet. There are stories of holy wells, flax mills, fairy forests and villages entirely obliterated by the Famine hunger. Initially, it's through low-lying fields and woodland paths before the route suddenly dives into the wildest of Mayo countryside. Rural and raw, it's genuinely unsanitised pilgrim terrain but excellent signposting ensures we eventually re-join tarmac.

The Tóchar Phádraig was a paved chariot road leading 72 miles from Rathcroghan, the seat of the Kings of Connaught in what is now Co. Roscommon, to Cruachán Aigle, the ancient name for Croagh Patrick, which even in pagan times was venerated as a sacred mountain. Later, Saint Patrick is reputed to have Christianised the route as he passed along it on his journey to Croagh Patrick. According to the Book of Armagh, which was written in the 8th Century, Saint Patrick tarried long enough on the mountain summit to build a place of worship there. In some collaboration of this account, an archaeological excavation in 1994 proved that an oratory built in the early Christian period did exist on the summit. Soon after Patrick's journey, pilgrims, drawn by the promise of Christian immortality, began to follow that same road to Ireland's holy mountain and over time the route became known as the Tóchar Phádraig or St Patrick's Causeway. These days most pilgrims climb Croagh Patrick in about 3 hours coming from Murrisk to the northeast of the mountain, but we are following the ancient route and this is set to take about 10 to 11 hours.

Down the road, arrows point us to the wild flower rich banks of the Aille River, which remain much as they were in ancient times, when pilgrims passed this way in search of spiritual immortality. Ascending to higher ground we are immediately rewarded, for filling the horizon is the symmetrical quartzite cone of Ireland's holiest and handsomest hill. Undoubtedly a moment of joyful epiphany for fatigued medieval penitents; for day explorers like us it's a place to take our obligatory selfies.

As we continue, the thought occurs to me that Medieval pilgrims must have been a uniformly tough bunch. Regularly, they must have felt isolated, lonely and vulnerable to robbery, kidnap and even death. And yet, whether motivated by escaping damnation or gaining eternal reward themselves or for a loved one who had passed away, they persisted, driven on each day by the need to reach the sanctuary of a monastery or an inn before nightfall. This was, of course, a simpler pre-Reformation time when virtually all of Europe was unified with one purpose; the glorification of God.

Gradually we settle into the metronomic but strangely comforting rhythm of walking, with almost every wood, lane, mass rock and stream we encounter seemingly laden with a saga from earlier times. Here it occurs to me that modern life has virtually killed the concept of travel; we are now rushed by mechanical transport from one place to another with little concept of the actual distance involved. On a pilgrim path, however, we experience the landscape in its true proportions. We pass a poignant famine graveyard and great cliffs where the jewels of Connacht are reputedly secreted. Later, the path traverses a deserted village before gaining the viewing point of Cloondachon Hill and descending into the pretty little village of Aughagower. Here, on a monastic site, which is reputed to have been founded by St Patrick, there is a later medieval church and the remains of a 10th Century round tower. More importantly and unusually for a small Irish village these days, Aughagower boasts a shop with a pub to the rear. As one, the entire group tumble in to enjoy a pit stop.

With the dissolution of Irish monasteries such as the ones at Aughagower and Ballintubber following the English Reformation, the Tóchar fell into disuse. It was almost totally abandoned when penal laws were enacted against Catholics. Remaining silent and almost forgotten for 400 years, it was the coming of Fr Frank Fahey to Ballintubber Abbey that was the driving force behind its re-awakening in 1988. It was also the first stirring in Ireland's modern pilgrim era.

Speaking earlier with Fr Frank, he told me something of his life story. Born near Ballyhaunis on the Roscommon/Mayo border in 1936, his father was a farmer and his mother a teacher. Educated at St Jarlath's College, it was here he developed a passion for Gaelic Football and was a member of the Mayo minor football team that won the All Ireland Championship in 1953. Having studied at St Patrick's Training College in Dublin, he subsequently worked as a primary schoolteacher in the capital. Entering the seminary as a late vocation to Maynooth in 1968, his studies coincided with an era of great change in the church, which he describes as "some of it good, some bad". Always his own man, he had some influence on changing the Pontifical University for the better; he was part of a successful strike that did much to improve the conditions for clerical students.

After his ordination, he was briefly appointed to Inishbofin Island which he loved because of its rich heritage and abundant folklore. Then, he was transferred to a place that was literally a world away; for two and a half years he was part of the United States mission. On what many would describe as a dream appointment, he was based between New York and Sunset Boulevard, Los Angeles. Here, he worked as a programme organiser for famous rosary priest,

Fr Patrick Peyton, who was also a native of County Mayo. A media superstar in his day, Peyton was close to many of the Hollywood glitterati such as Raymond Burr, Bing Crosby and Lorretta Young. One of the first to use the mass media to promote the benefits of family prayer for all religions, his catchphrase was "The family that prays together stays together".

After returning to Ireland in 1976, Fr Frank was appointed as curate to the Marian shrine at Knock, Co. Mayo. He spent a decade ministering there with the legendary Monsignor James Horan. This he describes as a very exciting time with the centenary celebrations for the Shrine, the building of the huge new Basilica of Our Lady and the coming of Pope John Paul II in 1979. He recalls being at the famous breakfast in the Parochial House in 1980 that followed the anniversary mass which celebrated the Pope's visit. This was attended by government ministers Pádraig Flynn and Albert Reynolds and was to immediately make another Irish upland famous. This was the occasion where Irish Taoiseach Charles Haughey promised the wily Monsignor Horan what he thought was a tiny grass airfield for Knock. Soon after, the Monsignor publicly unveiled plans for an international airport capable of handling trans-Atlantic jets on an upland site that was located over 200m above sea-level. Jim Mitchell, of opposition Fine Gael party, famously described the airport as located "high on a foggy, boggy, hill" but it was too late for Haughey to back out of his promise. With the benefit of hindsight, this has proven a good thing; Ireland West Airport has since proven an invaluable lifeline for Mayo and the surrounding counties and now handles about three quarters of a million passengers annually.

Next in his series of high-profile postings, Fr Frank was transferred to Ballintubber. The Abbey was already well known nationally having been restored and roofed in time for the 750th anniversary of its foundation, in 1966. The Tóchar Phádraig had, however, returned to almost total obscurity, with its last recorded use being in 1588. It was then used by Richard Bingham, President of Connacht, as a convenient pathway for his army heading for Aughagower to punish the rebellious Burkes for giving succour to the survivors of the Spanish Armada.

With his legendary enthusiasm and energy, Fr Frank immediately set about restoring the final section of the route from Ballintubber Abbey to Croagh Patrick. There were 64 landowners involved along the 22-mile trail and all gave consent to the restoration of the path, despite the fact that they received no monetary compensation for this. "It was a time of extremely high unemployment in Ireland" explains Fr Fahey, "and the farmers were delighted to help. We had 15 of the very best people on a FÁS (community employment) scheme who had been let go from their jobs. They did great work on the route and we opened in 1988. We were then very glad that the first pilgrims to walk the Tóchar in modern times were a group of Irish army officers, led by Coronel Michael Walsh."

He doesn't mention it himself, but it appears abundantly clear to me that it was Fr Frank's speedy actions after arriving to Ballintubber that ensured the survival of the Tóchar as a pilgrim route for the modern era. Had he not made moves in the mid-1980s to re-open the route, it is doubtful if it could be done in today's litigation and insurance conscious age. Certainly, he was surfing a wave with the Tóchar as the highly formalised belief systems of the 20th Century gave way to the more informal and individualised spirituality of the 21st Century, that commonly expressed itself through pilgrim walking.

Since the re-opening, Fr Frank has seen a big increase in the numbers walking the route. "In the beginning, we just had local people, but now, with the great expansion of pilgrim walking, the Tóchar has become much more popular. Most days in summer we have groups or individuals setting out from the Abbey to walk to Croagh Patrick. The majority are Irish, but we are also seeing more Europeans and Americans as the word gets out that completing this prehistoric route is a truly worthwhile experience. For those attempting it in a day, it is a tough 35km, but people are also completing it in a more manageable two days, with some local B&Bs dropping walkers out to the start and collecting them in the evening."

Subsequent to the re-opening of the Tóchar, the next major event at the Abbey took place in 1997 when the chapter house and dormitories were restored under the direction of Fr Frank. It is this area that is now used to cater for the thousands of tourists, pilgrim walkers and retreat participants who come each year to an Abbey that has simply refused to die.

Beyond Aughagower, we descend fields and join a road as the terrain changes noticeably. At its essence, pilgrimage is, of course, just meditative walking and it immediately seems to me that the landscape here is eminently suitable for a contemplative experience, since it is mostly on serene, tree-lined little roads that we make our final approach to "the Reek". Diving briefly into the surrounding countryside, we come upon the Boheh Stone, a pre-historic scene of druidic worship that was reputedly a massrock for St Patrick. Here we are amazed to discover it is in the back garden of a derelict house. Everyone immediately agrees that this important heritage site should long ago have been purchased by the State and the eyesore dwelling demolished.

One last excursion through fields and a crossing of the Owenwee River brings us to a tiny road skirting the overwhelming emptiness of Croagh Patrick's south face. Continuing along this and crossing the Western Way, we reach a base for Mayo Mountain Rescue and a last unwelcome sting in the tail. Here a switchback path leads steeply upwards to join the modern Pilgrim Trail on Croagh Patrick, it is tough going at the end of the day but eventually we reach the saddle between Crott Mountain and Croagh Patrick. This was our "wow moment" for into view came the great sweep of Clew Bay and the lordly Nephin Mountain beyond. Then, leaving an attempt on the summit of Ireland's holiest mountain for another day, we follow, as passport pilgrims are required, the trail downhill to the journey's weary end at Murrisk on the shores of Clew Bay.

Those finishing the Irish pilgrim journey then head off to have their passports stamped for the final time while the remainder of us enjoy a self-congratulatory coffee in Campbells atmospheric pub while secure in the knowledge we have, like penitent's past, defeated distance to complete the Causeway of St Patrick.

Having pondered this issue on my walk, I questioned Fr Fahey when I finally got back to Ballintubber Abbey, about what he believes is the motivation to embark on a pilgrim journey in the modern world. "People are taking up the pilgrim challenge in the 21st Century for two reasons," says Fr Fahey. "First is the modern trend towards incorporating walking the outdoors as part of a healthy lifestyle. But, on a more profound level, people are searching for a deeper meaning that the material world is not giving them. They are finding meaning, instead, within the simple but fulfilling experience of walking an ancient mystical path. These paths provide the space and the ambience to explore and, perhaps, find that which gives wholeness to their lives."

Never one to sit on his laurels, Fr Frank has, at the time of writing, obtained planning permission for the reconstruction of the East Wing of the Abbey. Showing me around the site, he hops from one foundation stone to another, while I puff along in his wake. Then he stops and points. "This will be an Interactive Learning Centre, exploring the pilgrim paths and centres of study since the beginning of time that have contributed so much to human identity, heritage and culture. The theme of the new centre will be the pilgrimage journey which has been there since the dawn of humanity. It will be titled 'footprints in the Sands of Time' and one of its most important themes will be the story of early pilgrimage to and from Ireland."

"Ireland was an important centre for pilgrimage in the early Christian period. We had people from across Europe coming to centres of learning like Clonmacnoise and Glendalough, while saints such as Columbanus and Gall went in the opposite direction to spread the gospel. Pilgrimage is the great historic bond linking us with the Continent. I believe the time has come to tell the story of how early Irish monks transformed Europe when it was devastated by invaders. We expect the Interactive Learning Centre will make Ballintubber an international centre for monastic tourism."

Later, after leaving the Abbey, I discover that one happening in his life story has been omitted. What he modestly refrains from telling me is that in 2016 the legendary curate of Ballintubber Abbey was inducted into the Mayo Hall of Fame alongside the former Irish Taoiseach Enda Kenny. One thing is certain, nobody can accuse Fr Frank of not having lived a full life.

# CHAPTER 11

# The Final Discovery

On the morning of 27 February 1987, a Kerry man in his twenties and a 16-year-old-youth were roped together beneath Ireland's highest mountain at a place known locally as the Heavenly Gates. They attached ice climbing crampons to their boots, which give extra purchase by cutting into the snow and ice with sharp points, and then began moving cautiously up the steep and snow-covered east face of Carrauntoohil.

Leading the climb was Con Moriarty, who was universally known in Kerry as the "Mountain Man". Born in the nearby Gap of Dunloe he came from a family with a two-century long tradition of guiding visitors on the Macgillycuddy's Reeks that began with his great-great-grandfather who was also named Con Moriarty. Proud of this family tradition, Moriarty explained of this period, "When my great-great-grandfather started guiding it was mostly for visitors to the great houses. It was at a time of obscene poverty in pre-famine Ireland when many more people were forced to live high on the Reeks. There were people living in the Hags Glen who just about survived by growing oats and potatoes."

In his book, *The Way that we Climbed – a History of Irish Hillwalking, Climbing and Mountaineering*, author Paddy O'Leary describes Moriarty as a big man, who was even larger in temperament and was vivid in expression. He also stated "Moriarty was easily the most colourful of the Kerry climbers. His love and knowledge of the hills, under which he was reared, was undisguised and an article he wrote for the *Irish Mountain Log* is the most authoritative essay written by an Irish mountaineer about his local hills and the people who inhabit their fringes." For a piece written by this author in *The Irish Times* 9/9/2006, Moriarty poetically stated of climbing, "There is nothing like the sensuous rhythm of climbing upwards on warm rock; rockclimbing at its best is a beautiful dance in wonderful surroundings."

An unwavering individualist, Moriarty didn't always endear himself to the east coast climbing community and tended to follow a line that was independent from the conservative Mountaineering Council of Ireland (MCI). Dedicatedly doing his own thing in the Kingdom, the six-foot five-inch Moriarty had singlehandedly done much to ignite and then improve rock-climbing in Co. Kerry. Along with a small group of like-minded pioneers, he went on to open up many new climbing routes on the north and northeast faces of Carrauntoohil, which up to then had been considered a no-go area on the mountain. A team leader with Kerry Mountain Rescue for over 10 years who had been instrumental in improving the technical skills of the members, he had, in 1983, made the first ascent of the hardest route to Carrauntoohil's summit. This was the distinctive line of Primroses Ridge, rated very severe in climbing terminology and dramatically separating the north and northeast faces of the mountain.

A lifelong explorer of the world's great mountain ranges, he had, the previous summer, travelled to Wyoming in the USA for a successful ascent of the Devil's Tower - a famous 265m pinnacle of vertical rock. Now, he had just returned from a winter climbing expedition to Scotland. On Ben Nevis, he had been enthralled by ascending the world-famous Tower Ridge in snow and ice conditions. Scotland had, of course, a historically strong tradition of ice-climbing. The ephemeral nature of snow on the mountains of the southwest of Ireland meant, however, the sport was virtually unknown in Kerry. Moriarty was now anxious to prove that challenging ice-climbing could also be found in Ireland and the severe winter of 1987 provided the perfect opportunity.

When, in late February, excellent snow conditions presented themselves, Moriarty wasted little time. Youthful climbing enthusiast John Cronin lived in nearby Mealis, where his home had for generations been the principal starting point for Carrauntoohil ascents and the usual base for the Kerry Mountain Rescue whenever the team was called to this mountain. The teenager was literally roped up at short notice for a winter attempt on the then little-known east face of the mountain.

Soon the pair were heading up the famous Hags Glen, which is surrounded by all of Ireland's highest mountains. They then veered away from the traditional "tourist route" leading to Carrauntoohil's summit and approached instead the, then little known, Heavenly Gates area beneath the northeast face of Carrauntoohil and began climbing from here. Despite the fact that both climbers had been born in the shadow of the MacGillycuddy's Reeks, they were now venturing into territory that was largely unknown to them. As the pair moved upwards from the Heavenly Gates, they were astounded to find themselves on a well-defined and challenging sandstone ridge no one had climbed previously.

One of several ribs now known as The Bones, the ridge they were on had remained unclimbed because - unlike the famous Scottish ridges - it is not easily identifiable from the glen below. Even today the line of this "shy ridge" is discernible only to those who know exactly where to look. Also, the old red sandstones of Kerry were then considered too friable, vegetated and loose by the - mainly east coast based - rock-climbing fraternity in Ireland at that time. The result was that few of the leading Irish rock-climbers of the day ever ventured to Kerry, preferring to make the drier granites of the Mournes and Wicklow their main playground.

According to Con Moriarty, "The local people didn't, in general, have recourse to the Reeks, mostly it was those coming to Kerry as visitors that would do so. The mountain climbing community that was in Kerry at the time was also quite conservative. They tended to stay within the realms of hillwalking and rarely ventured onto technical routes, so much of the local mountains remained unexplored. There is little doubt that had their ridge been located in, for example, the English Lake District where there was a strong tradition of rock-climbing, it would have been discovered and ascended a least a century earlier. The Kerry hillwalking community was, at the time, simply too small and inexperienced to allow a full exploration of the mountains."

Certainly, it is true that up to the 1980's there were really only three main routes used by hillwalkers ascending Carrauntoohill: The Hydro Road to the west; the Gap of Dunloe route to the east and the Hag's Glen track from the north. The principal walking guidebook at this time did not, for example, even mention the now hugely popular O'Shea's Gully route to Carrauntoohil's summit. It wasn't until a small groundbreaking guidebook to the Iveragh Peninsula was written by geographer Barry Keane in 1997 and published by Collins Press, that the vast untapped possibilities for climbing in the McGillycuddy's Reeks became generally apparent. This would be much later and for the moment Moriarty and Cronin were largely ploughing a lone furrow.

Moriarty took the lead on what turned out a mixed climb: this is where some of the route is over snow and ice and some is over bare rock. The pair were also "on-sighting" the ascent, which, in climbing terms, means doing it without any foreknowledge. This can be tricky, since climbers have no idea of the difficulties which may lie ahead and this kind of climbing has sometimes been likened to working out the solution for a complex puzzle. In this case, Moriarty led the climb by jamming pieces of equipment, known as wires, into cracks in the rock or putting slings around the larger boulders. A safety rope was then attached to these, which was secured by Cronin, whose job was to hold a fall. Skilled in this kind of climbing, Moriarty didn't fall as the pair made their way upwards over the snow-covered rocks.

The special features of the route now began to unfold and it became apparent that in many ways the climbing was superior to Tower Ridge. Clearly, it was harder and also, unlike the renowned Scottish ridge, it rarely relented but presented a continual series of intriguing challenges. Many times, the ice-crusted way ahead seemed barred by great benches of vertical rock, but somehow ice axe holds and purchase for crampon points always seemed to present themselves when required and so upward progress was maintained. On the first ascent the pair - unlike most climbers today who bypass some of the hardest obstacles - stuck rigidly to the pure line of the ridge. This considerably increased the difficulty of the ascent. Both were, however, doing extremely well and so the difficulties presented were not unduly troublesome.

Moriarty remembers "the characteristically rapid height gain of the area, the immediate grandeur and the magnificent scenery of our parish and beyond". Soon the climbers were above the Tower - which has since become recognised as the most difficult part of the route - and traversing a great slab of left slanting rock, which has since become known as The Bridge. Then, the pair were distracted by piteous howling from below. Moriarty's dog Grimsel had followed to the foot of the ridge. An experienced mountain climber, Grimsel was already a familiar sight on the Kerry Mountains as he accompanied Moriarty almost everywhere. This meant he had been to the top of most of the high mountains in Kerry including Carrauntoohil. On this occasion, however, he found the going - on what has since been graded a very difficult rock-climb - beyond even the considerable climbing abilities of a Pyrenean Mountain dog.

As the lonesome howling from a highly unimpressed Grimsel continued, the route veered right and suddenly the climbers found themselves in familiar territory. They had joined the top of

Primroses Ridge and from previous experience knew the way ahead to the summit was unobstructed. Incredible as it seems, they had - in the late 1980s - stumbled upon a previously unknown geographical feature of Ireland's highest mountain. It offered almost 300 metres of near vertical ascent and was promptly named Howling Ridge by Moriarty in honour of Grimsel - the mountain dog that didn't climb but howled piteously instead.

The final section of the climb, although appearing rather intimidating, is actually quite amenable. Over a couple of easy pinnacles and through a small gap and they were then free to unrope, having completed the Ridge. Afterwards, they swung south on steep ground, then east and downhill through an area known locally as Leaca Bhán (the white slabs). Here, they picked up the route leading to the Heavenly Gates, where they re-united with a doubtless relieved Grimsel before returning down the Hag's Glen to Cronin's Yard.

When I followed in the footsteps Con Moriarty and John Cronin about 15 years after their first ascent, I instantly fell in love with this great ridge. Unlike many of the routes on Carrauntoohil, Howling is generally a clean and unvegetated 300m ascent and so gives for very satisfactory and sometimes even exhilarating climbing. It begins tamely enough, but the intensity gradually increases and then rises to a great crescendo at the Tower before finishing with aplomb over exposed but relatively easy rocky pinnacles and a final small gap in the ridge line.

East facing, it catches the morning sun and so dries quickly. The result is that on sunny days when the mountain is in friendly mood and the sandstone offers excellent friction, climbing Howling provides a heart-raising feeling. This comes with rising rapidly heavenward on a superb face with Ireland's highest mountains all around and the austere beauty of the famous Hags Glen with its twin lakes laid out far below.

Having ascended the Ridge about a dozen times, I have also discovered that in a venomous mood, it can lay many traps to snare the unwary. The consequences of simple mistakes made by some climbers have varied from extremely serious to fatal. Isolated on Howling in poor weather with wet rock all around, it can also appear one of the loneliest and most intimidating of places, for it is difficult to escape or retreat once established on the route. Before taking on Howling it is, therefore, important to remember that if you can't continue your climb to the top of the ridge, it is most likely you will need rescue.

On one occasion I was part of a foursome who completed it in full-on winter conditions and, to my surprise, I found that it demands the same level of concentration and skill as required by many of the great Ben Nevis ridges and takes much longer to complete than might be expected. Afterwards, I remember reaching the top of the Devil's Ladder on a glorious moonlit night – it had taken us about 2 hours longer than we had predicted. All this means that Howling Ridge is an undertaking only suitable for experienced climbers, well used to coping with exposed situations and the vagaries of Kerry weather. In snow and ice conditions it should only be the playground of those with Scottish winter or Alpine experience.

Howling Ridge is today generally regarded as Ireland's finest mountaineering route, with some considering it the best climb of its grade on these islands. Its renown has spread, with the result that it is ascended hundreds of times annually by both Irish and overseas climbers. Originally undertaken as a winter climb, the infrequency of true winter conditions on the Reeks means it is now much better known today as a summer route. By no means the most difficult ascent on Carrauntoohil, it will, nevertheless, for almost any true mountaineer prove by far the most enjoyable. "Have ya done Howling yet?" is a common "getting to know you" inquiry in Irish mountaineering circles. Indeed, the ridge has become a rite-of-passage ascent for many hill-walkers eager to make the transition from mountain rambling to the knee-knocking intensity of scrambling and dangling off rock faces. Even Moriarty has expressed himself surprised by the popularity of this shy Kerry Ridge and has since stated "I had no idea coming off the Ridge that day that Howling would gain the popularity it has and that our climb would still be remembered and talked about 40 years later".

At the time of writing, John Cronin was the senior fire officer for Kerry Airport and proprietor of Ireland's first dedicated climbers' café and accommodation centre, which is located at Cronin's Yard beneath Carrauntoohil. His love of the mountains still manifests itself as a long-serving member of the Kerry Mountain Rescue Team and an Alpine climber. One of his fondest memories, however, remains his first climb of Howling Ridge. But didn't he feel nervous as a relatively inexperienced 16 year old heading off in winter conditions to a virtually unknown area of Carrauntoohil? The answer is an emphatic, no. "You always felt safe with Con; my parents never worried when I was with him. He was technically excellent but also was extremely careful, probably the best mountaineer I have ever been with."

After the Howling Ridge ascent, Con Moriarty continued his lifelong infatuation with mountaineering. In both winter and summer conditions, he put up many new climbing routes in Kerry for the love of the sport but never bothered recording most of them as other climbers do. He also climbed abroad in Nepal, Kenya, Indonesia, Australia, Patagonia, and New Zealand. His biggest undertaking outside of Ireland was a ground-breaking expedition to the beautiful Himalayan peak of Ama Dablam in 1991. It consisted mainly of climbers from the southwest of Ireland and, to the consternation of the MCI, was organised independently by Moriarty, who dealt directly with the authorities in Nepal when arranging the climbing permits. This was also the first introduction to high altitude climbing for Cork man Pat Falvey who would go to reach the summit of Mount Everest by both the Tibetan and Nepalese routes. Later, he would become the first person ever to complete the Seven Summits – the highest mountain in the seven continents - on two occasions.

With his usual meticulous attention to detail, Moriarty carefully planned every aspect of the climb, which involved using siege tactics – the creation of an ascending series of camps on the mountainside. Laid low with food poisoning, he didn't, however, make it to the summit, but, climbing alone, Corkonian Mick Murphy reached the top of the 6,812m Himalayan Peak after a tortuous ascent. At the time, Ama Dablam created a new record for the highest summit reached by an Irishman and did much to pave the way for the successful Irish expedition to Everest in 1993. One unfortunate outcome of the expedition to Ama Dablam was that a simple slip led to Con Moriarty sustaining a severe spinal damage, which would greatly circumscribe his future career as a climber.

Moriarty spent most of his life working as an incoming tour operator for Ireland and also followed in a century old family tradition of guiding groups on his beloved MacGillycuddy's Reeks. In 1986 he established Hidden Ireland Tours offering bespoke experiences of Ireland to small groups to overseas visitors. He fondly remembers the mid-1980s as a golden age for Kerry mountaineering and particularly for climbing on Carrauntoohil. "Not only did we discover Howling Ridge, but the severe winters of this period allowed a group of enthusiasts to put up a plethora of wonderful new ice-climbs on the north and east faces of the mountain that are now recognised as classics that will stand the test of time."

# CHAPTER 12

# Daily Defying Death

"It was just another day of climbing on Atlantic sea cliffs in Ireland with Mike [Reardon]. We had arrived on Valentia Island in a slight fog and drizzle. Mike took me around the bottom of Wireless Point to an inlet merely 15 feet above the roaring Atlantic, a situation we were now used to. We arrived at a spot he had climbed at alone two weeks prior. Mike up and downed two different climbs while I shot photos trying to combine him and the raw force of the waves crashing all around us. He finished the two climbs and was waiting, on an algae covered platform, for the big swells to pass by so that he could walk back over to me on the opposite side of the inlet. A rogue wave came into the inlet and curved rightwards as it crashed into Mike. He tried to stabilize himself on the platform but the water was too powerful and sucked him in. The current pulled Mike out 150-plus metres in mere seconds."

*– Damon Corso, photographer.*
*Quoted by climbing.com, 15/05/2007*

Michael (Mike) Reardon was a renowned proponent of a cutting-edge sport known as free solo climbing. What you are required to do is simple. You find a sheer cliff, maybe 100 metres high and climb all the way to the top. And you don't bother with ropes or other safety equipment. If you fall off you "deck", a climbing term for hitting the ground. If it is early on in the climb, you have a sporting chance of spending the remainder of your life in a wheelchair. If you come off near the top you're doomed.

The sport of free solo climbing is in many ways akin to free-diving, which is a form of underwater descent to great depths that relies on breath-holding. Both proscribe the use of additional equipment including ropes or oxygen tanks and so it involves partaking of either diving or climbing in its purest and simplest form. Each discipline is, nevertheless, a mammoth psychological challenge – give way to panic and you are finished. And, to say the least, it is hard to stay cool when you know, if anything goes wrong, there is no plan B. In no other discipline is extinction so quick and certain if you make a mistake. In fact, so nerve wracking is every second of free solo climbing that it is sometimes difficult to get camera persons to even film it, for the danger of the climbers sudden demise is always present terror.

The reasons to avoid such activities seems irrefutable, yet both disciplines attract a surprisingly large coterie of participants. One reason, I suppose, is that we live in an increasingly anodyne world where every effort is made to eliminate even the slightest risk from our lives. Many children are no longer allowed walk to school, run in a playground, climb trees or play cops and robbers. Adults can't carry shampoo onto an aircraft or buy more than two packets of paracetamol.

Indeed, if legendary explorer Captain James Cook lived today, he would most likely have failed to circumnavigate the world. A bureaucrat would surely have appeared at the quayside as he was about to set sail and listed a multitude of reasons why the Endeavour could not be licensed to transport human cargo. Health and safety audits may have made our lives safer and more comfortable, but they have also made them less challenging and more boring.

Of course, there are still some free-spirited people who resolutely refuse to accept the constraints that safety experts impose on the rest of us. Rock-climber Michael Reardon was one such person. American born, but of Irish ancestry, his paternal grandfather had emigrated from Co. Cork. Brought up on the East Coast of America, he later moved to California, where he lived, from an early age, the expansive and experience rich life common to those who eventually broaden the boundaries of human achievement. Always destined to follow the road less travelled, he was, in the 1980s, a member of a heavy metal band and later worked as a writer and film producer. He also had credited parts in films that featured A-list stars such as John Travolta and Helen Mirren.

Of independent means, having founded and then sold Black Sky Entertainment, a company that produced the hit movie *Cabin Fever*, he was in a position to devote himself fulltime to rock-climbing and documentary making. Having begun climbing on a boulder in his grandfather's back yard in California, he was soon moving on to harder challenges. Favouring free solo ascents over the traditional roped methods used by the vast majority of the climbing community, he immediately positioned himself as a climbing rebel with a cause. His explanation for taking the route less travelled was that initially he had no climbing gear or contacts within the sport - for free solo climbing you don't need a climbing partner to hold a safety rope or any special equipment.

Reardon was soon well-known for belonging to an elite group of top-level climbers - referred to as the Outlaws - whose members insisted on making ascents of huge cliff faces while unencumbered by safety ropes. To accomplish these ascents, Reardon spoke of putting himself into an eight-foot eggshell, where he was only aware of what was within a couple of feet in each direction and thus, he zoned out the huge drops below him.

The attraction for cutting edge mountaineers has always been the thrill of cheating death. The early pioneers did this by reaching the summits of the world's most iconic mountains, with many perishing on the way. When these had been tamed, the best climbers found new death-defying frontiers by following the most difficult routes to these summits – most famously the North Face of the Eiger, where failure meant inevitable death. Better climbing techniques and superior equipment means that many of these once awe-inspiring challenges have now been third classed and treated as mere tourist ascents. The new death-cheating frontier has now become free solo rock-climbing, for it taps into one of mankind's most basic and deep-seated fears – the terror of falling from a high place.

Reardon wasn't the first proponent of the sport, which had emerged mainly from California in the late 20th Century and was practiced mostly around the great granite cliffs in the Yosemite Valley of the Sierra Nevada Mountains. He was, however, one of the sports best-known and most colourful exponents. While most rock climbers will free solo climb when well within their comfort zone, Reardon was without peer in this realm, climbing long routes of up to 300m at a technical grade of up to 5.12c. This meant climbing vertical - or indeed, overhanging - cliff faces where the holds consist of small pinches and tiny "bird beaks". Reardon's free solo ascent of Romantic Warrior, a 300m route at this grade in California saw him awarded by *National Geographic* with the title Adventurer of the Year, 2005. This feat was not accomplished again until 2014 when it was repeated by world-famous, free soloist Alex Honnold.

For some people this method of ascent is climbing in its purest and most stylish form and has even been likened to artistic endeavour; to most others it appears foolhardy in the extreme. Unlike ocean racing or ascending the world's greatest peaks, where if things go wrong a possibility of survival exists, there is no chance of surviving a fall when soloing a high route. For this reason, there is an extended list of those who have fallen to their deaths while free soloing, and, as a consequence, the practice has long been controversial within the rock-climbing community.

Before we jump to conclusions, however, we should remember the age-old truism that those who dare to push back the frontiers of the possible are invariably considered foolhardy by their contemporaries. Despite the fact that tomorrow is promised to no one, public opprobrium was heaped on the first climbers to reach the summit of the Matterhorn, because of a tragic loss of life following an accident during the descent. It also fell lavishly upon the heads of those who died while doing battle with Switzerland's North Face of the Eiger in the 1930s, which was then regarded as a pointless waste of life. And in more recent years it has come upon women – but, noticeably, not on men - who have continued with cutting-edge climbing after the birth of their children.

Without people prepared to take such risks and drive themselves beyond their comfort zone, the world's greatest mountains would remain unclimbed, European explorers could hardly have reached America and the lunar dust would remain footprint-free. A relentless search for advancement is a key element of the human condition. If a challenge exists, then sooner or later somebody possessing raw courage beyond what the vast majority of us can comprehend will want to take it on.

Operating under the motto "We only get one shot at this dust ball", Reardon was such a person. Brash and outspoken, he wasn't everyone's cup of tea, but then those who strive hardest for perfection are rarely shrinking violets. Seldom understated and a natural showman, Reardon was a master at attracting publicity for his accomplishments. To the consternation of purists, he regularly left mementos, such as plastic figures of animals, on the rockfaces he climbed, while one stunt involved climbing a route while naked. A lover of the minimalist approach to rock climbing, he stated in an interview with the Irish Mountain Log magazine in 2005 "The truth is that barefoot, onsight, chalkless [without using chalk for drying sweat] climbing is pure climbing – everything else is a compromise."

On his many visits to Ireland, he hit the conservative local climbing scene like a tornado. Spurning long-held conventions on safety, in a country where free-soloing on hard routes doesn't really exist as a separate discipline, he took on many of this country's most difficult routes. "I have never been a middle of the road sort of guy. It is too easy and causes complacency." This is how he described himself and so it was little wonder that soon he was undertaking a pilgrimage around almost all of Ireland's most iconic climbing locations: Fair Head, The Burren, Ailladie and Glendalough, before fetching up at Kerry's famous Gap of Dunloe on his third visit.

Irish climbing had never quite seen anything like it. Describing free solo climbing as "a life wish, not a death wish", his standard climbing uniform consisted of Superman shorts and bright T-shirts, which sometimes morphed into a Cork GAA jersey. Occasionally, he went against all accepted convention by climbing in jeans. In many ways he was pure Hollywood come to Irish climbing. With his long tresses flowing in the wind and his easy and elegant style of climbing, he was totally unmissable, with his climbing style once described as "poetry in motion". Local climbers watched in astonishment as the blond "Californian wonder boy" glided unprotected up cliffs without using ropes and modern safety equipment. Award-winning Kerry photographer, Valerie O'Sullivan, worked as a photographer with Reardon for some of his climbs. She remembers him as "a larger than life character who was a total non-conformist. He was great fun to be with and always restlessly looking for new challenges and experiences." According to the *Irish Mountain Log Magazine* (Winter Edition, 2007) "the 240 routes he soloed in Ireland included the first ascent of the Rainy Days (5,12 +) at Ailladie" (Co. Clare). This is still regarded as one of the hardest climbs in the Burren, even for those using ropes.

Despite his daredevil reputation and the fact that as a fulltime professional climber there must have been continual pressure for new achievements, Reardon was never reckless in his approach to climbing. Those who watched him in Ireland invariably commented on his extremely cautious and calculating methods and on the fact that he scrupulously avoided taking foolhardy or unnecessary risks; he would back off a climb if he considered the risk too great. In a business, which is sometimes described as working hard to cheat death for another day and where one mistake almost invariably proves fatal, it just isn't possible to behave otherwise.

Once in Kerry, Reardon particularly wanted to visit Skellig Michael. According to photographer Damon Corso, who accompanied him on his Irish visit, he had earlier taken a boat tour out to the island and felt a deep spiritual connection with the rocks and the idea of the monks climbing up and down to the monastery hundreds of years ago. He was desperate to get a shot (photograph) on a particular crack that he had seen; the weather, however, refused to co-operate.

It was Friday, July 13, but Reardon was not seemingly concerned by any ill omens. Reardon and Corso were scheduled to accompany photographer Valerie O'Sullivan to Skellig Michael. The island was again stormbound, so the trip was postponed until the following day. Meanwhile, the alternative became a trip to the isolated and exposed Reenadrolaun Point at Dohilla. This consists of an exposed finger of land jutting into Dingle Bay from the north coast of another Kerry Island, Valentia. So ancient are the rocks at Dohilla, they contain the famous Tetrapod footprints created by an amphibious animal almost 400 million years ago. These were laid down in mud which then transformed into the siltstone that preserved the first known footprints on dry land from a time that long preceded the age of dinosaurs.

Reardon and Corso made their way onto the island that Reardon was never destined to leave. The selected climbing area was known as the Black Cliff. Although the climbs here were much shorter than Reardon was used to in California, they carried some additional risks. Very challenging and difficult to access, the rock platform at the base of the cliff is known by the islanders for its sudden tidal surges. Climbers are advised by locals to exercise extreme caution when operating there, and particularly when there is a high spring tide, as there was on this occasion. Later Corso recalled, "It was intimidating. But I'd gotten so used to being so close to the ocean at this point I just brushed any fear off."

It was from this place that Reardon was swept out to sea after his final climb of the day, while standing on the rock platform beneath the cliff. Corso immediately grabbed a 60m rope but the irresistible power of the ocean meant Reardon was already well over 100 metres out to sea. He then shouted something that Corso couldn't understand.

The photographer checked for Reardon's phone but, in the confusion, could not find it in the bag. He then shouted he was going to get help. According to Corso, "I ran up the hill to the Valentia Coastguard Station which is located about a mile away. Mike was still conscious in the water when I left him. The Coast Guard arrived on the scene no more than 15 minutes after the incident. Mike was nowhere to be seen at this point." Where minutes before there had been a vibrant human being, there was nothing now but an eerily empty ocean.

According to the *Irish Examiner* newspaper, Reardon's phone then rang and Corso picked up. The name of Reardon's wife Marci popped up.

"Marci?"

"Damon, why are you answering Michael's phone?"

Unable to break the nightmarish news, the photographer merely replied:

"Ah, Marci, umm, I'm going to have to ring you back."

Corso eventually managed to compose himself sufficiently to dial Marci and break the awful news.

"Marci, Mike's missing. He's been taken out to sea."

12 volunteer rescue boats, a coast guard lifeboat and a helicopter were on the scene that evening. Rescue services worked until dark but they found nothing. On Saturday, more coastguard boats and divers from the Naval Service combed the area, with searchers also scouring the shoreline. A helicopter with an infrared scanner, combed the area on Friday and Saturday, but the exhaustive search led to nothing. When the open ocean claims a victim, it rarely leaves evidence behind. Michael Reardon was never found and he has since been presumed drowned at sea. In the cruellest possible way, the Atlantic had denied a final closure to his wife and daughter.

When I visited the scene of the tragedy over a decade later, it immediately seemed a place where the visceral forces of nature were at their most potent. Travelling down the Ring of Kerry, I had hardly noticed a breeze, but once I passed the coastguard station and arrived to Dohilla I found myself struggling to stand against a gale. Atop the cliff at Reenadrolaun, I noticed the sea would become deceptively calm for a period. Then a wave would suddenly crash on the rocks below and wet me slightly while sitting 30m above the ocean. It was at once magnificent and scary, but I could see why Reardon was drawn here: it is the perfect place to get close and personal with the rawest and most untamed forces of Ireland's Atlantic Coast.

Not surprisingly, many people in the media instantly concluded that the world's best-known solo climber of the time had finally overreached himself and that his disappearance resulted from a climbing error, with initial reports suggesting he had fallen 10 metres into the water. The reality was more mundane; he had been taken by the ocean when the climbing had been completed for the day and he was standing on a rocky platform, which many would have considered a safe distance above the ocean.

Five days later, about 150 people attended a ceremony at Reenadrolaun Point to mark the tragedy. Reardon's wife Marci and teenage daughter, Nikki, had flown in from California for the event. There was music, prayers, poetry and tributes, with members of the coastguard placing a wreath in the sea. The attendance included Kerry mountain running champion John Lenehan and legendary Gaelic footballer, Mick O'Connell.

Fr Kevin McNamara, from Killarney led the prayers. Reardon, he said, had pushed things to the limit. A ship was safe in the harbour, but that was not what ships were for. A plaque reading "Inspirational free climber" and "An solas geal lonrach" (bright, shining light) was then placed at a spot above where he was swept out to sea. Carved from local slate, it was hewn at the Valentia Slate Quarries which lie directly above Reenadrolaun.

Certainly, Reardon will long be remembered as an often-controversial figure, who, nevertheless, brought adrenaline rich ascents and high-profile glamour to rock-climbing. With the body of a rockclimber, the striking looks of an Instagram celebrity and the soul of a poet he was born, perhaps, a tad too early. There is little doubt he would have prospered hugely had he been around to exploit the boundless opportunities afforded by the social media age - free soloist Alex Honnold had, at the time of writing, 1.7 million Instagram followers. As it was, Reardon's artistically flowing technique on the greatest rockfaces placed challenges that would have been considered outlandish, even ten years earlier, firmly within the frontiers of the possible for future generations of climbers.

And, in the end, one of his predictions in an interview came poignantly true, "I don't intend to die climbing".

# CHAPTER 13

# The Call to the Mountains

Around 8am on 26 December 2017, Alan Wallace set off to climb Carrauntoohil, accompanied by his brother-in-law Ger and 18-year-old son, David. A long-standing tradition exists in Kerry of climbing to the roof of Ireland on St Stephen's Day, but this morning Wallace found the mountain hushed and almost deserted. Deep snow blanketed the MacGillycuddy's Reeks while the weather forecast was predicting further deterioration; this had deterred the usual horde of holiday-time walkers from attempting Ireland's highest mountain.

His group was well prepared for winter climbing. A long serving member of Kerry Mountain Rescue Team (KMRT), he was an experienced mountaineer with an intimate knowledge of the terrain. Ascending by a route known as O'Shea's Gully, the threesome summited around noon and immediately encountered rapidly worsening weather. An icy gale whipped across the snowfields, while a whiteout had descended on the mountain. Disorientating and dangerous, this is where it becomes impossible to distinguish earth from sky.

Soon enveloped by a full-on blizzard and with no visible landmarks, they were forced to navigate by map and compass only. Wallace recalls, "These were some of the most challenging conditions I have encountered on the [MacGillycuddy's] Reeks. The snow was waist deep in places, visibility was virtually zero, a storm was raging and the cold was intense."

Also on the mountain that day was Jim Ryan, author of the

definitive guidebook: *Carrauntoohil & MacGillycuddy's Reeks*. Here is his account of the conditions he experienced. "We climbed via O'Shea's Gully. Half way up the gully it started to snow. We had reached the top of it when the blizzard started. It was safer to proceed to the Cross [summit of Carrauntoohil] than to retrace our steps. At the Cross there were eight others. Three of them were young lads in runners. Everybody there headed off to descend down the Ladder [The Devil's Ladder route]. The wind was driving the snow into our eyes so that, without goggles it was impossible to see. We had to descend the Ladder on our backsides, stone by stone. All the way down the Ladder the wind continued to drive the snow into our eyes."

Well-equipped and experienced, Wallace's group descended safely off the mountain. They were making their way towards the car park and the promise of food and an evening with family, when out of the gloom loomed the KMRT rescue vehicles. Clearly, someone was in trouble.

A sophisticated and highly trained organization today, Kerry Mountain Rescue Team arose from humble and tragic beginnings. At a time when Ireland was preoccupied with celebrating the 50th anniversary of the 1916 Rising, Myles Kinsella, a student from UCD, set off alone for an Eastertime ascent of Ireland's highest mountain. Tragically, he died in a fall on the east face of Carrauntoohil. This area was then little known and almost entirely unmapped which meant his body remained undiscovered for several months. Soon after, a member of an English school party was also killed in much the same area of the mountain. He fell while the group was traversing from the west side of Carrauntoohil towards the Hags Glen. In the absence of a local mountain rescue team, the remains of both climbers were recovered by rescuers who had travelled from Dublin.

In the light of these sad events and with increasing numbers having recourse to the Kerry Mountains, Frank Lewis of Cork-Kerry Tourism decided that action was needed. In July 1966, he assembled a team of volunteers willing to provide search and rescue services to those in difficulty on the slopes of Ireland's highest and most technical summits. These volunteers were drawn mainly from the newly-formed Laune Mountaineering Club in Killorglin.

Early members included well-known racing cyclist Paddy O'Callaghan, Stan Brick, Gearóid O'Sullivan and Richard Morrison from Killorglin, along with Terence Casey and John McGuire from Killarney. The first task came in November 1966, when the newly formed team assisted in the recovery of the remains of Myles Kinsella, who had died seven months earlier.

The following year, the skills of the new team were tested rigorously. Cork man Bill Collins was climbing on the steep and unmapped eastern face of Carrauntoohil when he fell and was seriously injured. His companion, Con Horgan, then descended to seek help, which was the only way to raise the alarm in those pre-mobile phone days. The inexperienced team members were then faced with rescuing Collins from a remote and most dangerous location.

The all-night rescue that followed from the vertiginous mountainside, which has since been denoted Collins' Gully, still remains one of the most demanding epics of the team's history. With a storm raging, it required eight perilous hours in stygian darkness to lower the casualty and a further three to carry him to an ambulance.

The rescue team spent 19 hours on the mountainside without food and in the worst possible conditions. Later, rescuer Paddy O'Callaghan recalled, "The terrain was desperate and we had no helmets and only minimum equipment. We could have been killed or injured ourselves but the mission was a success and we went on from there."

This experience showed that providing a volunteer rescue service on the unforgiving mountains of Kerry and West Cork was no place for well-intentioned amateurs. Instead, it required mountaineers with geographic, technical and medical competency. These competencies were greatly enhanced in 1973. It was then Bill Marsh, chief instructor at Glenmore Lodge (Scotland's National Outdoor Centre), was invited to provide a week-long training course for KMRT volunteers in Glencar. This was extremely valuable in providing the team with an awareness of the latest cutting-edge search and rescue skills.

In contrast to the informality of the early years, mountain rescue was becoming a complex undertaking. New competencies, particularly in the area of ice climbing, were severely tested during the harsh winter of 1986. In February a young doctor fell to her death while descending from Carrauntoohil in icy conditions. While members of KMRT were recovering the remains from the snow-covered mountainside, news came through of three experienced climbers who had been avalanched in an area known as Curved Gully on the North Face of Carrauntoohil, which had only recently been climbed for the first time in winter conditions.

Avalanches are relatively rare in the Irish Mountains, but they do happen occasionally when there is a sufficient build-up of unstable snow. Denis O'Connell, who was a member of the avalanched party explained afterwards that the drama started at around 4pm on Saturday when he and his two companions had almost reached the summit of Carrauntoohil. "All of a sudden, an avalanche of loose snow came down on top of us and we were swept down a gully", he continued. "We were actually on a bed of snow and could do nothing to help ourselves. We must have fallen about 1,000 feet", said O'Connell. Luckily, their plight was spotted by a Dublin climber named Tom Murphy, who was out photographing the snow-covered mountainsides. He heard their shouts for help and by 8pm was off the mountain and had raised the alarm.

Kerry Mountain Rescue Team dispatched an advance party which included Con Moriarty, Mary Walker, John Cronin, and Tom Murphy. They set off in the darkness and came upon the injured climbers around 1am, close by the shoreline of Comeenoughter, the highest lake in Ireland. The advance party remained with the casualties throughout the long winter night, while two further rescue teams were sent up during the hours of darkness including KMRT volunteers, Stephen Thompson, Kevin Tarrant, Mick Barry, Pat Quinn, Tim Long and Jan Van Soes. Since the casualties could not be airlifted from Comeenoughter, it was necessary to get them further down the mountain through a series of hanging valleys. Formidable climbing skills were then required to lower the casualties down a frozen waterfall from where they could evacuate by helicopter. According to Moriarty, "at that stage, there were only six ice axes in the whole of Kerry and that night we used every one of them."

A rescue from the air could not take place until daylight and an Air Corps helicopter arrived from Baldonnell, Co. Dublin at 9am. It quickly picked up the injured climbers, who had just been laboriously lowered to a secure place from which they could be winched up. All the casualties were safely transferred to Tralee Hospital with relatively superficial injuries and made a full recovery.

Recalling the incident, Moriarty stated, "advanced ice skills were used for the first time to evacuate the casualties". This, he believes, was a seminal time for mountain rescue in Kerry. "In order to fulfil our commitment to providing the best level of service possible we were forced to reassess our standards. It was now agreed that only those with pre-existing mountain skills would be recruited into KMRT. Formal training would concentrate on the transmission of mountain rescue techniques only." This has been the position ever since. All team members now undertake specialised training courses designed for outdoor rescue. They are also expected to maintain a high level of physical fitness and to provide much of their own protective clothing and equipment.

A bizarre controversy arose soon after, that could quite accurately be described as the storm in a water tank. At the instigation of Con Moriarty some members of the rescue team, with assistance from members of the local hillwalking community, decided to build a mountain hut high on Carrauntoohil. The idea was this would act as a base for climbers and also as a refuge for those unable to descend from the mountain in difficult conditions. Created from an old water tank, the hut was covered with stone and then topped with grass to make it practically invisible.

Moriarty's initiative did not, however, go down well in Dublin. Heated words were exchanged with the Mountaineering Council of Ireland who demanded its removal, claiming the modest edifice was in fact, the highest building in Ireland and required planning permission. Not a man that could easily be dictated to, Moriarty refused to remove the hut. Soon after it became an accepted part of the local landscape and universally referred to as the Mountain Rescue Hut.

Almost immediately it was to prove useful during a search for an English computer programmer, John Harradence, who disappeared on Carrauntoohil while climbing alone in September 1989. KMRT members were able to remain overnight in the hut, which greatly facilitated an extensive search that sadly proved of no avail. Harradence's remains were eventually found six months later having been washed down a gully on the east face of the mountain by springtime floods.

In December 1998, an epic involving five Dublin teenagers camping high on Carrauntoohil would again prove the value of the decision to build the hut. A storm blew down their tent and they spent the night shivering in survival bags. One teenager knew about the rescue hut and at first light managed to lead the others there, which probably saved their lives. Tired and suffering from dehydration and cold they sent the two most able members of the group down to alert KMRT, while the remaining three were protected from the worst of the cold by the hut.

Realizing that speed was essential and that another night on the mountain would prove lethal, the rescuers began a hasty ascent in conditions that local Garda Sergeant, Pat Lehane described as "a desperate day, in fact, the worst in my lifetime". At one point conditions became so bad the rescue team thought they would be forced back, but they persisted knowing lives could be at stake. When they finally reached the youths, they were suffering from severe exposure and needed to be warmed-up in the hut before they could be safely taken from the mountain.

That night the teenagers slept unharmed in their beds but there was to be no rest for the rescuers. The following day two women became lost whilst descending Shehy Mountain in appalling weather and were enveloped by darkness. A preliminary reconnaissance by KMRT managed to pinpoint their location but they could not be reached directly because of severe flooding. The rescue team was obliged to make its way over Tomies Mountain on the darkest of nights. To reach the pair they forced their way through the densest of undergrowth in weather conditions described by long-serving rescuer Mike Sandover "as absolutely atrocious – we had to carefully mark the route in, otherwise, even the rescue team might not have found its way back out". Finally, guided by radio communication from other volunteers who were watching from a vantage point, the women were eventually located and escorted to safety.

The 1998 rescue of the deputy editor of a British magazine titled *The Great Outdoors* (TGO) - who was visiting Kerry to write an article about walking in McGillycuddy's Reeks - also concluded happily. John Manning certainly got a more dramatic piece of writing than he had bargained for. With a female companion, he took the wrong route of descent from Carrauntoohil and the couple was forced to spend an appalling night shivering in a survival bag. Failing to arrive as planned at the Climbers Inn in Glencar, the alarm was raised at 1am.

After an exhaustive full day search by KMRT that started at first light, the couple was eventually located just before nightfall. They were sheltering in a gully beneath the precipitous Beenkeragh Ridge, which leads to Ireland's second highest mountain. After being given food, warm drinks and dry clothing, they were then walked off the mountain. Writing later about the rescue in TGO (November 1998) Manning stated, "we were made to feel like paying guests by the guys [KMRT] whose professionalism, friendliness and genuine goodwill belied the fact they were all volunteers".

Of course, not every call-out ends heartwarmingly. When reports were received, in January 2002, that three climbers had fallen in a gully above Lough Dubh, which is in a remote area of MacGillycuddy's Reeks, a rescue team was immediately airlifted to the scene by the coastguard. An injured person, found beneath a steep gully, was evacuated by helicopter in gathering darkness. A treacherous night search of the gully then confirmed every mountain rescuer's worst nightmare: the two other climbers had perished. Rescuers stayed with the remains throughout the long, cold January night and next morning began the harrowing task of lowering the bodies. So inaccessible was the area, the remains of the two climbers had to be transported across Lough Dubh by inflatable canoe to reach a suitable place for airlifting.

So, how do the volunteers cope when they encounter such harrowing fatalities? Con Moriarty says, "mountain falls are by their nature violent affairs and the victims are not a pretty sight, making it difficult for rescuers to maintain the emotional distance necessary to do a professional job. And this becomes almost impossible when, as sometimes happens in the small world of climbing, the victim is known to the rescuers." Mike Sandover agrees and adds, "such victim recoveries are by far the most traumatic for mountain rescue teams. Individual counselling is now available in such cases, and group sessions are also held where the rescuers are trained to watch for symptoms of post-traumatic stress disorder."

In the half-century since the Kerry Mountain Rescue Team was founded, much has changed in terms of equipment, search management, first aid technology and climbing competencies, alongside a huge increase in the number of recreationists having recourse to the uplands. Certainly, the area has become Ireland's most popular upland playground. In particular, Carrauntoohil and the McGillycuddy's Reeks have together morphed into a huge visitor attraction. In 2018, 140,000 recreation seekers entered the area from the 4 main access points, with the sheer weight of numbers greatly adding to the responsibilities of the rescue team.

Modern technology has, of course, helped. In the past, mountain rescue teams were generally called out when someone failed to return from the hills; this very often involved a night search. Now with mobile phones, KMRT generally become aware of an incident soon after it happens and will have a rough idea of the location. A big advance here has been the Sarloc smartphone application, which enables rescuers to pinpoint the location of individuals who are seeking assistance if an internet signal is available from the casualty's phone. This sometimes acts as a huge labour saver for the team, but like most pieces of technology, it does not always work. When this happens, the alternative is still a manual sweep which is one of the most labour intensive and demanding tasks that can face a mountain rescue team.

One modern invention that appears initially to offer huge labour-saving potential in mountain rescue situations is drone technology. It is easy to imagine teams avoiding a laborious volunteer search by sending a drone up the mountain with a camera to identify the location of a lost walker or casualty and then sending the rescuers directly to them.

Like most other things in life, however, it isn't quite that simple. KMRT have acquired a drone but, at the time of writing, conditions had never been right for its use. According to Colm Burke, of KMRT, "Drones can be useful in some situations, the quick delivery of food, clothing and medical supplies to those marooned on a mountainside. There is no substitute, however, for having a team of fit, dedicated rescuers who are immediately available to respond to a mountain's emergency. They can give reassurance to those in trouble, remove them safely from dangerous locations, assess the nature of any injuries and stretcher the casualties off the mountain if necessary. I think there will always be a need for human input when it comes to assisting those who find themselves in trouble in the uplands."

Certainly, there has been, over the years, lots of interaction between walkers in difficulty and KMRT volunteers in the uplands of the Southwest. After its foundation, the Kerry team was the one with the most annual callouts in Ireland until the hillwalking boom of the 1990s made the Wicklow rescuers busier. The large area of operation and the challenging nature of the terrain means, however, that the demands on the KMRT team remain considerable. As an example, the team had 44 callouts in 2018 that involved seven fatalities and required a contribution of 4,440 volunteer hours by the 35 team members drawn from many walks of life.

All volunteers are now qualified in Advanced Rescue Emergency Care and first-aid training continues regularly to maintain the skills of each volunteer and enhance them. There is also ongoing training in a range of other specialities such as casualty care, ropework, stretcher lowers, cableway rescues, helicopter winching, search management, navigation and radio communication. One fact has remained a constant however, no one being rescued has suffered any further injury once delivered to the care of the rescue team.

The KMRT area of operation covers the entire southwest of the country – principally the peninsulas of Beara, Iveragh and Dingle – which contain 15 of Ireland's 20 highest peaks. Since its foundation, the team has remained deeply rooted within the communities in these areas. Mike Sandover speaks of the special relationship it has with local people. "When we have a long-drawn search and rescue operation, householders inevitably throw their doors open to us. I sometimes believe there isn't a loaf or a slice of ham left in the base valley when the time comes for the team to stand down. A rescuer never goes hungry in Kerry." This close relationship is further emphasized by the fact that about 50% of the KMRT's annual budget comes through private donations and the Team's own fundraising efforts within the community. Such endeavours must be supported by all team members and so KMRT volunteers are a regular sight fundraising on the streets in Kerry towns.

Throughout all the changes over the years, one factor has, however, remained unaltered; the Kerry mountain rescue service is provided on a totally volunteer basis with KMRT members not even receiving travel expenses when using their own vehicle to respond to a callout. According to Mike Sandover this is now unusual. "On the European mainland it is almost a totally professional service." Yet, despite the growing demands and lack of remuneration, there is never a shortage of volunteers to take up the rescue mantle. In times of full employment and diminished volunteerism, this shows an extraordinary commitment to a task that is often dangerous and traumatic, while never anything but physically demanding.

When Alan Wallace and his two companions finally reached the rescue team on St Stephen's Day 2017, the news was that a climber had become lost on Carrauntoohil. Wallace immediately grasped the gravity of this; in the prevailing weather it would be almost impossible to survive a long winter night on open mountainside. It was imperative the climber be located quickly. Famished and cold after a long day, Wallace, nevertheless, joined his fellow volunteers in the rescue effort.

Having identified his location as somewhere on the southeast of the mountain, the climber was advised to stay put and await rescue. Several teams then headed out into the storm and began a laborious sweep search. Eventually, the casualty was located in deep snow near Carrauntoohil summit. Now enveloped by darkness, the team had to painstakingly assist him down for immediate transfer to hospital.

In the meantime, two other climbers reported they had also become disorientated while descending Carrauntoohil. A team was dispatched to their location, which was on steep ground approximately 400m above the Devil's Ladder. Now followed the physically demanding task of helping the climbers - who were showing the early symptoms of hypothermia – to descend the snow-choked and slippery Devil's Ladder.

One of the pair soon began losing sensation in his feet, so it became more urgent to get down for rewarming. Ploughing through the deep snowdrifts proved extremely demanding however. A fresh team, including Wallace, was dispatched to help the tiring rescuers. "It was tough going, but eventually, we managed to get the exhausted and dangerously cold climbers down for transfer to hospital," said Wallace.

As the team was about to stand down, a third emergency call was received. A high-altitude camper reported his tent had been destroyed by the storm. The exact location of the causality was unclear, with communication difficult on a poor phone connection; then the signal died.

Working on scant information, the most likely position appeared to be the Black Valley side of the Reeks. As much of the nation celebrated St Stephen's night with family and friends, the team transferred to this isolated area and commenced a sweep search by torchlight that continued into the early hours of December 27th, but to no avail. According to Wallace "searching for a casualty on a dark, stormy night without location coordinates is like looking for a needle in a haystack". That night Wallace reached his home in Killarney at 2.30am. His sleep would be short, however; the search resumed at 8am.

With its renowned fickleness, the Kerry weather now bestowed a crystal-clear morning. A rescue helicopter could be safely deployed, and soon the camper was located. Winched from a ridge - known as The Bone - he was transferred to hospital, while the team members recovered his belongings, before returning to their families in the late afternoon.

Next day there was another callout that came just before midnight. A group of three climbers reported that one of them had fallen 10m and broken a leg on Carrauntoohil's Howling Ridge. Evacuating a casualty in ice and snow conditions from the ridge - which is graded very difficult - would involve a highly technical operation. After discussion, it was decided to postpone the evacuation until morning. An advance party of two was dispatched in the interim with food, warm drinks, spare clothing and first aid to stabilise the casualty and prepare for rescue at first light.

This party consisted of KMRT volunteers Piaras Kelly and Aidan Forde. According to Kelly: "It was a horrendous night when we set out; the rain was bucketing down. This meant it was snowing heavily at altitude. Luckily, it began to clear as we climbed and eventually, we could pick out the three headtorches."

"Reaching the group about 3am, we found they had already moved off the ridge. Assessing the injury, we concluded the leg was not broken, so it was possible to assist the group to Carrauntoohil's summit. We then decided to short-rope them down by the Devil's Ladder", explained Kelly.

Just when all seemed under control, the mountain played its final card; the rescuers were enveloped by a severe thunderstorm. Kelly recalls, "Lightning flashes lit the mountains like daylight and thunder rolled. Carrying steel ice-axes we were petrified, but there was nothing that could be done. We just continued bringing the casualties down."

The storm passed, but, in a final cruel twist, Kelly badly sprained his ankle when he stepped into a hole concealed by the deep snow. "I was in agony, nearly as bad as the casualty. Another couple of volunteers had to be called, but eventually we managed to reach safety and dispatch the casualty to hospital as dawn broke. Then when I took off the boot, my ankle was like a balloon. It took months to heal, but the success of the rescue made the pain worthwhile," concluded Kelly.

Christmas 2017 was a tough and physically demanding time for KMRT, but nobody in the team complained. The important fact was that eight people had been rescued with nobody seriously injured. This is what counts as a happy Christmas for the members of the hardworking rescue team, who very often find themselves heading up the mountains on a call-out in conditions that would have all sensible people coming off. In a self-absorbed age, they still remain a bastion of selfless volunteerism and community service.

# CHAPTER 14

# The Living Rockscape

I scrabbled around for a crack to place a piece of gear for protection, but you weren't in any mood to cooperate. Nothing presented itself which was serious; without some protection in place I could neither continue to the top nor lower to the base of the climb. There was urgent need for a secure placement to jam in a piece of equipment called a nut. This would hold the rope in the event of a fall and stop me hitting the unforgiving boulders far below. I was uncomfortably aware that there would be no contest between my bones and your hard, coastal limestone, but the face you presented remained smooth and inscrutable. Literally caught between a rock and a very hard place, I had become what climbers call cragfast, unable to move either up or down. The situation was delicate to say the least, but there were climbing friends nearby. Forced to admit that you had defeated me, I ignominiously called for a second rope to be lowered to secure me from above while no doubt you were grinning at my feeble effort.

In your vertical world fear is always a light sleeper and, on this occasion, you had managed to scare the daylights out of me. At other times you have, however, delighted, enthralled and, I fancy, made light-hearted fun of me. Indeed, it baffles me how anyone could fail to experience a frisson of excitement at the siren call of your high karst-lands. I have certainly found them irresistible over the years, for yours is an area of pure geological theatre. No matter how often I come, there is always a renewed challenge or something fresh to explore. Invariably my eyes are drawn to some place I didn't notice before or to a new boundary which must be conquered, for nowhere else in Ireland is so much enchantment shoehorned into such a confined space.

Born in the bed of a warm shallow ocean over 300 million years ago, you made your entrance to the world at a time when Ireland was located near the Equator. These oceans teemed with life and gradually shells, bones, plants and animal remains were deposited along with sediments on the seabed. Over millions of years these hardened into limestone and became you. Colliding continents and unimaginable earthquakes then pushed you above the ocean and into the visible world, where further collisions forced the limestone upwards to create your vertically unassuming but hugely contorted mountains.

Soon after, the continents broke apart from each other and Ireland began its long journey north to its present location. On arrival in the mid-latitudes you settled - luckily for Irish tourism - comfortably as part of the Irish west coast. At that stage, we wouldn't have recognised you, for you were still wearing your dull brown overcoat of shale; your striking beauty had yet to emerge. Erosion gradually stripped away some of your outer clothing and you began to reveal your true nature. Helped by the coming of several ice ages, when great glaciers scraped away much of the soil and shale, the result bestowed a delightfully polished limestone bedrock. It was the soft Irish rain that eventually completed the job. Slightly acidic, it dissolved your porous limestone skin over time and created your uniquely permeable expanse of exposed carboniferous pavement that is often referred to as lunar landscape.

You were now beginning to look like the Burren we know and love, but, of course, elbow grease was required to smooth your face and keep you that way. Hazel and ash thrive in limestone areas and in the newly temperate climate these began to envelop your pavements. To your rescue came Stone Age farmers about 6,000 years ago. Normally it is the arrival of humans to an area that marks the beginning of problematic environmental practices. These farmers were, however, helpful to your cause by felling the trees and clearing much of the scrubland. Doubtless, they were then surprised to discover that cattle thrived on your seemingly austere face, for scattered amongst the pavements is some of the most fertile grazing land in Ireland. The relatively intensive agricultural practices of these early farmers prevented the natural forestry from recolonising your bare landscape. The modern paradox of your being is that otherwise unsustainable practices, such as the intensive over-grazing of the early farmers, are now being re-introduced to prevent your fragile ecosystem succumbing to its natural state as a monocultural hazel and ash forest.

Most upland farming systems incorporate some form of transhumance, which generally involves stock moving to the lowlands in winter. You aren't just any old upland, of course, and so a unique system of farming evolved to meet your special requirements; livestock are moved from the lowlands to the hills as winter approaches and are then brought down again in springtime. One of your talents is obviously animal husbandry as you thoughtfully provide what farmers would badly want for their livestock "a dry lie". Your limestone pavements are extremely permeable and so water quickly seeps away through the vast network of underground streams and caves. Cattle lying within this embrace are dry and comfortable. The karst also absorbs heat from sunshine and releases it slowly. It offers cattle a type of storage heating that helps them thrive in winter while offering the added bonus of a longer growing season. From the farmer's point of view, it is also a very efficient system – no expensive sheds for over-wintering livestock are required and the amount of extra feed needed is minimised.

In return for their bed and board, livestock do their bit to provide the great diversity of plants and flowers for which you are world famous. They graze the winterages very close, which means that the vegetation is sparse coming into spring. Wildflowers then emerge in profusion during the springtime without having to compete for light and nourishment. In the absence of cattle, your floral displays thrive without being trampled upon or grazed throughout the summer. And this is what has created the colourful meadows of wild flowers sprouting from fertile rocks to dance in a summer breeze.

It the sublime enigma of your being - in what appears a desert of stone, rare living things and captivating landforms abound. Unique to your face, Arctic, Alpine and Mediterranean flowers bloom side by side in beguiling variety. There are mountain avens, beautifully delicate orchids, bloody cranesbills and, of course, the startlingly blue flowers of the ephemeral spring gentian. According to the great naturalist, Robert Lloyd Praeger: "the result of the luxuriance and abundance of these (flowers) is that over miles the grey limestone is converted into a veritable rock-garden in spring, brilliant with blossom."

Then, there is the abundant evidence of past human endeavour that is scattered across your rocky landscape like a vast outdoor museum, for your past history was entirely written in stone. Still a fascinating work in progress that is continually mutating, you offer a farrago of richness for botanists, archaeologists, rock-climbers, geologists, walking enthusiasts and potholers among your fertile pavements. With summer gone you cannily manage to attract an entirely different demographic: lovelorn visitors come from far and wide to seek romance at the Lisdoonvarna Matchmaking Festival.

It was Shakespeare who said "one touch of nature makes the whole world kin" and this is certainly true in your case, for you have become an internationally branded rock-star drawing visitors to Ireland from across the globe. Yet, you somehow manage to retain your character, neatly accommodating traditional farming practices, which are little altered since ancient times, beside these visiting hordes.

I first fell for you on a coastal drive I embarked on as a teenager along your sublime coast road from Doolin to Ballyvaughan with a return over renowned Corkscrew Hill. Undoubtedly, this is one of Ireland's finest scenic routes, where you offer intoxicating views to Connemara and your three offshore siblings that form the Aran Islands. At the time I was suitably impressed, but this isn't the outing that truly floats my boat these days; when I want to us get close and personal now, I pull on the hiking boots.

One of my first Burren walks was the ancient pilgrim route over the Gleninagh Pass. On the trail, I remember reflecting that this wasn't so much a question of walking over you as with you. The trail you led me along is almost exactly as I had imagined the perfect penitential path. Here, was an evocative unaltered and serene upland experience like no other, offering the added bonus of striking views. There was also an inescapable sense you were trying to draw me somewhere; you were beckoning towards what lay beyond the horizon. And you didn't disappoint. Over the head of the pass, the trail offered an overwhelming sense of emptiness on the shoulder of Capanwalla Mountain – a photographer's dream of expansive views across the Burren landscape; it was intoxicating and I wanted more.

Soon, I was spending many a pleasant day exploring. One summer's morning, I rambled out from Fanore Beach and was soon after following one of the many green roads that wrinkle your rugged face. Originally built to facilitate the movement of livestock, the drovers using this route would have enjoyed the bonus of panoramic views over nearby Black Head. Eventually swinging southeast across your craggy limestone uplands, I kept having to remind myself that clints are pavements of limestone while grykes are the horizontal cracks that I had to keep stepping over.

One thing I liked about this outing was the way all human endeavour is represented with every successive era bequeathing a story that was written before me in rock. Even my untrained eye could pick out a mesmerising array of pre-historic enclosures, stone forts and cairns alongside the route. Passing the ancient fort of Caherdooneerish, it was clear that early farmers took advantage of the abundant local limestone to build this large edifice which would protect both themselves and their livestock within the security of a high place. Then, it was on over Gleninagh Mountain where the thought came to me that the unrelieved emptiness of your high karstlands would seem, to the uninitiated, a skeletal landscape filled with nothingness; in reality it secretes a treasury of complex flora.

Beyond Gleninagh, I headed across a great plateau that had been beautifully sculpted by nature to reach the stony remains of Caheranardurrish. In use until relatively recently, this occupies a more accessible and hospitable location compared with Caherdooneerish and so the local tradition that it once served incongruously as both a community chapel and pub carry a ring of credibility.

My outing concluded along a road, bisecting the magnificent Caher Valley, which is referred to locally as the "Khyber Pass". This valley carries the unique distinction of hosting the only Burren river that manages the considerable achievement of flowing above ground, so my return journey to the unique sand dunes at Fanore Beach was accompanied by the unfamiliar but musical sound of gurgling water. On arrival, wet-suited surfers were skilfully riding the fast, curling waves for which your west coast is justifiably renowned.

But everything isn't on the surface, of course, for you are a genuinely 3-dimensional landscape. Acidified rainwater burns easily through your limestone so rivers disappear with startling suddenness into great swallow holes. Reaching the impermeable rock layers on which you are laid, streams are formed that cut their way underground through the limestone above the non-porous layers. Over time these have carved out huge cave systems, which means that at your heart you are much like a huge Swiss cheese with 50km of cave systems having, so far, been mapped.

Adventure fanatic that I am, this fact was, of course, likely to draw me like a moth to light. I took to exploring your underworld; first with experienced potholers and later with friends. In many ways the cave systems you have created are the last frontier of the unexplored in Ireland. I was never likely to push back the boundaries of the known world, but I did discover that your underground caverns can run for miles.

As water dissolved through the roof of these caves over millennia, unimaginably beautiful stalagmites and stalactites and multi-coloured flowstones were formed. It proved a fascinating world, miles removed from that of show caves, where you gave desperately needed shelter to freedom fighters during the War of Independence and provided sanctuary for the last of Ireland's brown bears as the climate cooled before the Ice Age. Great caverns, waterfalls, colourful rocks and calcinated pillars of the purest white, that few other people have ever witnessed, were wont to pop up with startling brilliance. The whole experience was sometimes like walking into an impressionist painting until I turned off my headtorch. Then, it became an eerie place of Stygian darkness and overwhelming silence which was broken only by the metronomic sound of dripping water.

Unforgettable outings included Doolin Cave and the long knee-wrenching scramble to visit the greatest free-hanging stalactite in the northern hemisphere, which runs to a length of over 7m. These days you pay an entrance fee for this privilege, but I visited at a time before Doolin Cave became a major visitor attraction. Another outing that was invariably memorable to me was to the great underground waterfall in Poulnagollum when it was in full winter spate. A most impressive spectacle indeed, when accompanied in the confined space by the thunderous sound of a falling deluge.

Sometimes, you must have laughed at my puny efforts. In a personal Father Ted moment, I once led a group of friends into a dead end on a flat-out crawl where the cave roof was about 12 inches above our helmeted heads. I would hate to read their thoughts as they were then forced to make an ignominious backward crawl in an extremely tight space with you, I fancy, grinning and thinking "Could have told you so".

Other days, I came to partake of the abundant rock-climbing opportunities you offer. Some of great coastal cliffs, such as at the Cliffs of Moher, are magnificent to behold but quite useless for climbing. The shales, sandstones and flagstones of these great declivities are too loose and subject to rock fall to allow for safe climbing, even if it were allowed. But with almost infinite variety on offer, you compensate further up the coast. The relatively easy roadside crag at Ballyryan (pronounced locally as Ballyreen) was a favourite of mine. Here, I spent many a sunny day playing around on the rocks with friends, while passing visitors on the coast road stopped to photograph our antics.

In the afternoon, we would often move to the great cutting-edge cliffs at Ailladie, which were a totally different kettle of scary fish. These rise to 40m and consist of good, clean limestone that is, for the most part, terrifyingly sheer. Gamely, I had a go, and did manage to lead some routes at the easier end of the crag but even here we had our misunderstandings. One day, I fell off a climb and my weight dragged out a piece of protection from your soft limestone on the way down. The result was I toppled quite a long way before another piece of protection stopped me abruptly. The shock then dragged the much lighter individual holding my safety rope up to meet me on the cliff face, which was certainly a strange place to say hi.

Eventually, I moved to harder routes further along the cliff. In reality, I was out of my depth here, and so it came to pass that one day I found myself cragfast on your bosom - unable to go up or down. While waiting for a rescue rope to be lowered, you took pity on me, I fancy, and decided to cooperate. I spied a tiny crack into which I might get what is known as a small wire for protection. I jammed it in eagerly and it fitted beautifully. Rope attached; my ascent could now continue. After inserting another couple of wires for protection I dragged up my battered old body and toppled ungracefully over the top, collapsing in a sweating heap. It was then the rescue rope arrived, but blushes had been spared; I could claim a small victory.

Despite these occasional speed-bumps in our relationship, we remained close. Nevertheless, it took me a long time to discover the glories of Mullaghmore Mountain, the Queen of the Burren. Hidden away from the main tourist routes, this magnificent swirl of naked, gnarly limestone is the outstanding jewel even within your rich treasury. It came to prominence some decades ago when proposed as a site for a controversial interpretive centre. A firm believer that your story is best told on-site and directly by knowledgeable local guides, I was glad when intense opposition put paid to the project. It is the far-seeing opponents of the development we can thank for rescuing this rich, but fragile landscape from the damaging intrusion of modernity.

I remember particularly on a blue-sky July day some years ago, roving out towards the scene-stealing contours of Mullaghmore. Skirting the wild flower rich banks of Lough Gealáin that - it being summertime - were transformed to a symphony of colour, I then followed the arrows up the flaggy hillside. On the stout flanks of the mountainside, I passed a school group. The children were industriously examining the pieces of coral and fossilised crustaceans embedded within the rocks that are proof positive you began life beneath the ocean. Ruefully, I reflected, this was the type of "learning by exploring" which had been denied to those of us who grew up in 20th Century Ireland and were chained to the classroom desk.

As I followed the wandering paths on the south side of Mullaghmore, an isolated house to the west grabbed my attention. It couldn't be, or could it? Through the zoom of my camera, there can, however, be no doubt – this was indeed Father Ted's bleakly unadorned dwelling from the eponymous sitcom. And, as if to reinforce the veracity of this, I could discern groups of visitors photographing the lawn where Bishop Brennan rushed back unexpectedly from Rome to boot Ted in the direction of the Clare skyline.

On reaching the summit, intoxicating prospects, belying the modest elevation of just 200m, unfolded in all directions. Everything that is essential to your makeup was on view: the rounded hills flowing into each other, the intensity of colour, the islands of green, the chalk crusted lakeshores and the eye-wateringly bright terraces interspersing the limestone pavements that from every vantage merged in faultless harmony. Most eye-grabbing were the immense contours of folding limestone on Slieve Rua, which seemed intent on squeezing the very life from the mountain.

Then it occurred to me that when a Cromwellian officer named Ludlow described the Burren as "a country where there is not enough water to drown a man, wood enough to hang one, nor earth enough to bury him", he couldn't have been describing this part of you. Below me is a sweeping vista encapsulating not only your famous rocky moonscape, but also thriving woodlands and fertile fields where a body might easily be disposed of. There is also enough liquid to drown an entire army with this water lying mostly within turloughs: a landscape feature that is almost unique to you. These consist of small lakes, where the water comes and goes through underground passages and levels rise and fall with startling rapidity causing the lake to disappear entirely in spells of dry weather.

All this puts me in mind of the paradox around you: what appears to the uninitiated, such as Ludlow, a rocky wilderness is actually an immensely complex landscape. It contains many distinct habitats that can be a generous provider for those who know how to work with you and not against you. Unique to Ireland, you are indeed a gem but we must also strive not to become carried away with your splendour, for you are not Ireland's only bountiful landscape. Other, less show-stopping habitats have also contributed to our national survival: the rich cornlands of Wexford, the great dairy country of the Golden Vale and the raised bogs of the Midlands. All have, in their own way, made a historic and worthwhile input to national welfare and biodiversity.

To conclude this book, I returned to sample again the glories of Mullaghmore Mountain in a nostalgic trip down memory lane. An easy scramble deposited me beside the cairn on the summit where I had one of those moments when the world around me appeared to slow down and I felt part of the silence. Tarrying awhile, it felt appropriate that I should end my saunter through the history, folklore and legends of the Irish uplands in this place, for almost every historic age is represented on your weather-worn face. There is: prehistoric, Poulnabrone Dolmen; early Christian, Oughtmama Churches; Cistercian, Corcomroe Abbey; Tudor, Leamaneh Castle and 19th Century, home of Gaelic Athletic Association founder, Michael Cusack. You truly have a story from every era, but this is only decipherable by those astute enough to read the clues in your complex landscape.

Reflecting upon your timeless durability and permanence immediately reminds me of my own transience and triviality. You have been my escape from the travails of life, yet our relationship is an unequal one - the lifespan of a mayfly compared with an oak. Almost indifferent to time, you are over 300 million years old while, on a 24-hour clock, by contrast, I would have arrived to your bosom at a couple of seconds to midnight. Indeed, the entire human race must seem as strange ephemeral interlopers having noisily arrived to the party just a few minutes ago.

Yet, it would be remiss of you to underestimate us, for the human race now has the capacity to destroy in a short time the beauty which has taken you millions of years to create. Our future challenge is to resist the temptation to allow your face or indeed any part of

Ireland's upland inheritance to be irrevocably despoiled as the pressure intensifies from the ever-expanding demands of human need. Instead, we must adopt a long-term sustainable approach aimed at supporting the type of healthy interaction between humans and uplands, which has occurred for millennia across your haunting hills, benches and pavements.

# Select Bibliography

Breen, D. (1964) *My Fight for Irish Freedom*. Anvil Books, Dublin.

Barry, T. (1949) *Guerilla Days in Ireland*. Mercier Press, Cork.

Comerford, R.V. (1979) *Charles J. Kickham: A Biography*. Wolfhound Press, Dublin.

Carey, M. (2011) "Eamon an Chnoic" *Upperchurch Historical Journal* 2011, p.4-53.

Falvey, P. (2018) *Accidental Rebel*. Beyond Endurance Publishing, Kerry.

Harpur, J. (2002) *Sacred Tracks: 2000 years of Christian Pilgrimage*. Francis Lincoln Limited, London.

Killeen, R. (2012) *A Brief History of Ireland: Land, People and History*. First edition, Robinson, Great Britain.

Lawlor, C. (2003) *In Search of Michael Dwyer*. Chris Lawlor.

McGettigan, D. (2005) *Red Hugh O'Donnell and the Nine Years War*. Wolfhound Press, Dublin.

Moloney, S. J. (1952) *The History of Mount Melleray Abbey*. Paramount Printing House, Cork.

O'Cuinn, T. (2005) "Where does the Fugitive lie?" *Glenreemore or Glenmalure. Journal of Irish Mountaineering and Exploration Historical Society*, Volume 2, p.12-14.

O'Donnell, R. (1998) *The Rebellion in Wicklow*, 1798. Irish Academic Press, Newbridge.

O'Leary, P. (2015) *The Way That We Climbed: A History of Irish Hillwalking. Climbing and Mountaineering.* Collins Press.

Praeger, R.L. (1997) *The Way That I Went.* Collins Press, Cork.

Ryan, M. (2003) *Tom Barry: IRA Freedom Fighter.* Mercier Press, Cork.

Ryan, M. (2005) *Liam Lynch: The Real Chief.* Mercier Press, Cork.

## Want to keep reading?

Currach Books has a whole range of books to explore.

As an independent Irish publisher, dedicated to producing quality Irish interest books, we publish a wide variety of titles including history, poetry, biography, photography and lifestyle.

All our books are available through
**www.currachbooks.com**
and you can find us on Twitter, Facebook and Instagram to discover more of our fantastic range of books. You can sign up to our newsletter through the website for the latest news about events, sales and to keep up to date with our new releases.

currachbooks

@CurrachBooks

currach_books

CURRACH
BOOKS